B+ GRADES, A+ COLLEGE APPLICATION

B+ GRADES, A+ COLLEGE APPLICATION

How to Present Your Strongest Self,
Write a Standout Admissions Essay,
and Get Into the Perfect School for *You*—
Even with Less-than-Perfect Grades

JOIE JAGER-HYMAN, EdD

TEN SPEED PRESS
Berkeley

Copyright © 2013 by Joie Jager-Hyman

All rights reserved.
Published in the United States by Ten Speed Press, an imprint of the Crown
Publishing Group, a division of Random House, Inc., New York.
www.crownpublishing.com
www.tenspeed.com

Ten Speed Press and the Ten Speed Press colophon are registered trademarks
of Random House, Inc.

Library of Congress Cataloging-in-Publication Data
Jager-Hyman, Joie.
    B+ grades, A+ college application : how to present your strongest self, write
a standout admissions essay, and get into the perfect school for you / Joie
Jager-Hyman, EdD.
        pages cm
    Includes index.
1. College applications—United States. 2. Exposition (Rhetoric) 3.
Universities and colleges—United States—Admission. I. Title.
    LB2351.52.U6J34 2013
    378.1'616—dc23
                                                          2013004970

Trade Paperback ISBN: 978-1-60774-341-5
eBook ISBN: 978-1-60774-342-2

Printed in the United States of America

Design by Katy Brown

10 9 8 7 6 5 4 3 2 1

First Edition

To my A+ family:
Henry, Josh, Mom, Dad, Shari, Joe, Jonathan, Linda, Eddie,
Arlene, Jay, and Andrew

CONTENTS

ACKNOWLEDGMENTS

This book would not have been possible if it weren't for all the magnificent students and parents who have generously let me into their lives and who have trusted my counsel on the angst-ridden process of applying to college. I have been fortunate to work with truly wonderful families over the years and to see my students transition from intimidated high schoolers to confident college students to graduates who take the world by storm. I am filled with gratitude for all the amazing thank-you notes, holiday presents, flower deliveries, and generous referrals to friends. Thank you from the bottom of my heart.

I am also indebted to my writing mentors and friends. Laurie "best agent in the world" Abkemeier, there are no words to express how grateful I am for everything you do—your incredible editing, fresh ideas, and staunch support of my career as a writer. I wish I could write one hundred more books just so I could have you as my agent on these projects! Thank you also to the "famous writers"—Kate Torgovnick, Alex Morris, Ethan Todras-Whitehill, Felice Belle, Scott Lamb, Courtney Martin, Kimberlee Auerbach Berlin, Jennifer Murphy, Florian Duijsens, and Cristina Pippa—for being in my literary life all of these years, for encouraging me to write and sell, and for reading so many boring drafts about financial aid. Of course, this book would not exist without my smart and lovely editor, Lisa Westmoreland, who believed in the project and gave me all the support I needed to make it a reality.

I have been fortunate to have many mentors, but I must give a very special thanks to Sally Rubenstone, who said "yes!" when I officially asked her to be my mentor a couple of years ago. Sally, you are always,

always there to guide me with your clever ideas, swap war stories, bounce things off of, and warn me when I am heading in the wrong direction. Just having you in my life gives me the courage to take a risk as big as writing this book. I also want to thank my mentors from Harvard—Bridget Terry Long, Ellie Dargo-Severson, Mandy Savitz-Romer, Gary Orfield, and Ann Coles—who taught me that there is nothing more important than giving students access to college, and the people at the CollegeBound Foundation, who are on the front lines every day and are generous enough to give me a glimpse of their amazing work. Finally, thank you to the Dartmouth Admissions Office, both for admitting me all those years ago and for allowing me to help select students that came after me.

Finally, as is obvious from the dedication page, I am so grateful for my wonderful family. I never could have done this—or anything—without your support. Words cannot express how much I love you.

INTRODUCTION

Congratulations! If you are picking up this book, then you (or someone close to you) must be a high school student getting ready for college. Perhaps you have been anticipating and looking forward to this moment for years. Or maybe you find the thought of college visits, applications, essays, and interviews about as appealing as taking a math test "just for fun." Wherever you fall on the spectrum of college-planning excitement, rest assured that this book will arm you with the tools you need (including the occasional pep talk!) to land at the school that is right for you.

I have been helping high school students apply to college for over a decade. I first became interested in the application process after I graduated from college and took a position in the admissions office at Dartmouth, where I had been a student. When I left to attend graduate school a few years later, families began to approach me with questions about navigating the confusing maze of college admissions and financial aid. Since that time, I have shepherded many students and parents through the application process and have seen firsthand how stressful it can be. Some people think I am crazy for picking a career path that requires me to go through the college application process every year! However, I wouldn't trade one minute of it for the profound satisfaction I experience when my students are accepted to schools that will truly allow them to thrive. Every time I get updates from students about college experiences that opened doors for them, I know that all the application stress was worth it.

With competition for admissions to college at an all-time high, the media consistently publishes gloomy articles about how students need a perfect GPA or a perfect jump shot to get into a decent college these days. In turn, guidance counselors and college-prep books often focus on the academic superstars, the straight-A students who have their sights set only on the Ivy League. But what about the *good* students—the ones who go to class, do their homework, get good grades, and still want to have a life that doesn't completely revolve around school? What happens to students with Bs or even the occasional C on their transcript? If you are feeling disheartened or even doomed when it comes to getting into a good college, this book is for you.

WHO IS THIS BOOK FOR?

I wrote this book because I want every college applicant to have fantastic college options and the know-how to put together a winning application. Forget everything that you've read about how impossible it is to get into college these days. You do not need to be superhuman or well connected to go to a good school. There are literally hundreds of colleges for students like you just waiting to be discovered.

Is this book only for students with B+ GPAs? Of course not. When I talk about B+ students, I am referring to students who work hard and do well in school but may not have a "perfect" transcript or a 2400 on the SAT. These capable students sometimes feel discouraged by their guidance counselors or the media, even though they get good grades. You don't have to be in the running for valedictorian to complete a college application that shows what you have to offer.

HOW TO USE THIS BOOK

The following chapters cover everything a high school student needs to know about applying to college. I start by discussing some of the different paths that students take to find the colleges that are right for them—the best names, the best deals, and everything in between. Don't know what you want to study or what type of academic environment is ideal for you? Don't worry. This book has lots of advice on how to identify your college priorities and find colleges that will truly allow you to flourish. Want to go to an Ivy League school but don't think that a student without a 4.0 can get in? Relax. This book gives you the scoop on how to bypass the ultracompetitive admissions processes at schools like Harvard and the University of Pennsylvania through their under-the-radar programs, which are easier to get into, cheaper to attend, and still award you that big-name degree.

Once you have identified the full range of terrific college options at your disposal, this book will walk you through the application process so that you can understand how colleges make admissions decisions and how to maximize your chances of putting together an application that showcases what you have to offer. Confused about whether to apply early decision and early action? No clue how to write a compelling college essay? Need to painlessly beef up your extracurricular profile? If so, keep reading. These pages will answer all of these questions and more with helpful worksheets, questionnaires, and "action steps." The last chapter of this book also provides some tips for parents. The appendixes offer a detailed college admissions timeline for high school juniors and seniors, suggestions for getting into a top college through a "side door," and a list of colleges to consider.

Just because your transcript isn't perfect does not mean that you can't find the "perfect" college that will allow you to thrive. Let the journey begin!

CHAPTER 1

CHOOSE YOUR OWN (COLLEGE) ADVENTURE

Finding your Dream U. is like finding a great doctor, personal trainer, or significant other: it's all about compatibility. Some students start the college search process with strong, clear priorities, while others are more flexible or need time to decide what they want from a school. *No one path is better than any other.* If you grew up dreaming of becoming a meteorologist or a novelist, this book can help you find the best college to get you on that track. If you have no idea what you want to do with your life, do not panic. This book will guide you in finding colleges that can help you identify your passions while giving you a terrific, broad liberal arts education.

SIX DIFFERENT PRIORITIES, SIX DIFFERENT PATHS TO COLLEGE ACCEPTANCE

High school students today are bombarded with media stories about how valedictorians and class presidents are being turned away from top colleges in record numbers. If you're not at the top of your class, you might find yourself having regular nightmares about college rejection letters. To help you sleep better at night, I want to begin this book with stories of six students and the six different paths they took to find their dream schools. To protect their privacy, I changed their names and some personal details, but these stories are real. You may discover that you instantly relate to one of these students, or you may see parts of yourself in a few of them. Even though each student falls into a different category in terms of college priorities, they all rose above some flaw on their transcripts and ended up at a fantastic college.

PATH #1: THE BRAND-NAME SHOPPER

The title says it all: a *brand-name shopper* is someone who cares about labels—whether it's Calvin Klein or Columbia University. When it comes to choosing a college, brand-name shoppers prioritize a college's name recognition and prestige over things like size, location, and the school's particular academic departments. Brand-name shoppers are not necessarily superficial people; they simply believe that the best way to get a return on their college investment is to choose a school with instant name recognition. Though most students factor college rankings and other measures of prestige into their decisions, brand-name shoppers put the college's reputation above all else when making decisions about where to go to school.

Amy from Princeton, New Jersey, is a classic brand-name shopper. Amy begins her junior year with a 3.2 GPA at a competitive college-prep high school. She goes to class and generally does her schoolwork, but she also has been known to put the books away when one of her friends needs to talk after a big fight with her mom. Comments like "talks too much in class" and "easily distracted" have haunted Amy's progress reports since middle school.

Early in the second semester of her junior year, Amy meets with her guidance counselor to talk about possible colleges. She is crushed to hear how dismissive her counselor is of her chances at a great college because of her grades. For the first time, Amy feels emotional about her academics. She looks down at the list of colleges her guidance counselor selected for her—a blend of second-rate state schools and a few local, nonselective private campuses—and feels like the last kid to get picked for dodge ball. As her red eyes scan the tear-streaked piece of paper, a single thought repeats itself in her mind: *I am better than this.*

The next day Amy vows to turn things around. With her SATs four weeks away, she cancels plans with her friends and lets the phone ring in order to study. Her grades steadily improve and she finishes her junior year with more A-s and B+s than she ever got before. In June, she receives the results of her SATs: 620 in critical reading, 580 in math, and 560 in writing. Not terrible, but Amy knows that she needs to do better to get into a prestigious college.

Amy finds the answer to her prayers a few months later when hanging out with her neighbor Sandra, who is home from college during summer vacation. Sandra is about to start her junior year at Vanderbilt University in Nashville and has always been a strong advocate of going to a college with good weather. She asks Amy if she has ever heard of the Oxford College program at Emory University. According to Sandra, the Oxford College program is easier to get into than the other undergraduate programs at Emory University, but all of the students still graduate with the same prestigious degree.

Later that day, Amy does some research on Oxford College, located thirty-five miles from the main Emory University campus. The two-year program gives students a supportive, liberal arts education and allows them to transfer to the "regular" bachelor's degree program at the Emory College of Arts and Sciences and complete their studies on the main campus. Amy's heart starts to race when she sees the admissions statistics: 44 percent of applicants to Oxford College get in! Sandra was right—it is easier to get accepted to Oxford than to the Emory College of Arts and Sciences, even though these students eventually all graduate with a bachelor's degree from Emory University in four years. Amy immediately makes plans to visit the school.

Applying to the Oxford College program at Emory University makes sense for Amy because she is a brand-name shopper, and this program gives her the best shot at getting a prestigious degree. Luckily, Emory is not the only school with one of these "side door" programs. Many prestigious colleges—including Ivy League schools like Harvard, Columbia, and the University of Pennsylvania—have separate undergraduate programs with more relaxed admissions criteria than they use for their liberal arts students.

If you're a brand-name shopper, make sure to read appendix B, Getting into a Top College Through the Side Door, where I give the scoop on these under-the-radar programs.

PATH #2: THE SPECIAL AGENT

LeBron James, Bill Gates, and Lady Gaga all have one thing in common—they each identified a passion early on in life. While these people are cultural icons, you don't have to be a prodigy to have a passion. We all know people who profess that they were "born to be" something—the chef who grew up helping her mother in the kitchen or the doctor who loved volunteering at a hospital in high school. These people identified their dreams early and never deviated from that path. Similarly, the *special agent* is someone who approaches the college search with a clear, focused goal.

Julia, a student at Niles Township High School in Skokie, Illinois, is a great example of a special agent because she knows exactly what she wants to study in college. Ever since her first camping trip as a Girl Scout in elementary school, Julia has been enamored with the environment and has consistently dedicated herself to environmental causes. Among other things, she refuses to drink bottled water, shops almost exclusively at thrift shops, convinced her parents to update the insulation in their house, and can often be found going from room to room unplugging the appliances that are not actively in use.

Julia knows that she wants to be an environmental advocate and is open to professional paths in nonprofit organizations, public policy, law, or journalism. To prepare for any of these careers, Julie is looking for a college with a strong environmental studies department and a thriving green culture. In the summer before her junior year of high school, she decides to educate herself on her college options. One of the first things that Julia does is a simple Google search using the words *green campus*, which pulls up rankings from respectable organizations like the Sierra Club and familiar blogs like Treehugger.com. Julia instantly recognizes that some of the colleges on these lists—Harvard, Yale, Dartmouth, and Columbia, for example—are too selective. Others—the University of New Hampshire, the University of Vermont, UCLA, and the University of Colorado—are too big for her tastes.

Eliminating these two categories—the schools that are too selective and too big—leaves Julia with a manageable, preliminary college list that includes Oberlin, Hampshire, Bates, Smith, Bard, Lewis and Clark, and Reed. Robin, Julia's good friend from the Environmental Awareness Club, suggests that she also look at Mills College in California.

After she finishes up her final exams in June, Julia heads out to Oberlin where she really falls in love. The school is the perfect blend of passion and whimsy—where activists mix freely with the actors and singers. Julia can easily picture herself passing the hours at Oberlin's Adam Joseph Lewis Center, which is dedicated to green living and learning. Her eyes light up as she peruses the course catalog; at least a dozen environmental studies courses interest her, and the Oberlin faculty seem to be pioneers in the sustainability movement. The Ohio location also feels like a good match for Julia's midwestern sensibilities. Because Oberlin is selective, she realizes that she is going to have to do everything she can to submit the best application possible.

The next step for Julia—and for all students who want to maximize their chances of getting into their dream schools—is to do her best to make a connection with the admissions office and demonstrate interest in the college. There are many ways to do this, including visiting the campus overnight, signing up for an interview, attending information sessions when the Oberlin representative comes to visit her high school, and following up with a short, polite email to the admissions officer. The purpose of this personal contact is threefold: (1) by getting as much information as possible about the particular application process at her dream school, Julia will find out how best to present herself when she applies; (2) making a positive impression on the person reading her application won't hurt; and (3) colleges respond to students who make their passion for their campuses clear. Read chapter 3, Getting a Good Gut Feeling, for tips on how to make a personal connection with admissions officers.

PATH #3: THE ATMOSPHERIST

Aesop told a famous fable about the country mouse and the city mouse, describing how each mouse is suited to its particular environment. If they were high school students looking at colleges, these mice would be great examples of *atmospherists*, who prioritize the campus environment above all else in their college search. They absolutely know that they want to be in a certain type of school—a large, urban university like UCLA; a small, rural liberal arts college like Colgate; or a medium-sized suburban campus like Brandeis University. Or maybe they're huge sports fans who want a school with a big, packed football stadium on game day like the University of Alabama or Michigan State. Perhaps they want a particular educational philosophy, such as a women's college or an HBCU (historically black college/university). Atmospherists put the type and location of the school above all else in their college search.

Juan, a student in the top 20 percent of his class at a well-regarded private school in St. Louis, is a great example of an atmospherist. Juan lives in tight jeans, memorizes the weekly live music listings in the local alternative newspaper, and can provide detailed critiques of the art house movie theaters in town. Juan's dream school is NYU for obvious reasons. Unfortunately, while Juan has always been one of the top students in his English courses and is strong in history and French, he knows that his C+ in math is going to cost him at a top school like NYU.

Juan begins his search by listing colleges located in cities in which he could be happy for four years—New York is his absolute first choice, followed by Boston; Washington, DC; Los Angeles; and Chicago.

Here's his list of schools:

- New York: Columbia, NYU, Fordham, Hunter College
- Boston: Harvard, MIT, Boston University, Northeastern University
- DC: Georgetown, George Washington, American University
- Los Angeles: UCLA, USC, UCSD (University of California at San Diego), Occidental College
- Chicago: University of Chicago, Loyola

Because he is enrolled in mostly honors classes at a challenging, college-prep high school, Juan is hoping that his overall GPA will be looked at in context when it comes to the college admissions process. He also knows that being a Mexican-American might help him at colleges that are looking to enroll a diverse applicant pool. Though he hasn't yet taken the SATs, Juan is confident that he'll score well based on his PSAT results (640 on critical reading, 610 on math, and 700 on writing) and the fact that he has always been a strong test taker. Still, even if he nails the SATs, Juan rules out Columbia, Harvard, MIT, Georgetown, or the University of Chicago based on their selectivity. UCLA, USC, and NYU will each be tough, but he might have a shot if he can get his SATs where they need to be, writes a great essay, and gets stellar teacher recommendations. Juan's better bets include Hunter, Fordham, Boston University, Northeastern, George Washington, American, Occidental, UCSD, and Loyola.

When Juan meets with his guidance counselor to talk about a preliminary college list, his counselor suggests that he also look at the University of Miami in Florida. Though he had never considered Miami, Juan likes the size and feel of the school when he visits over spring break. He decides to apply to NYU early decision and to the University of Miami early action, figuring that he will hopefully have one college acceptance by December of his senior year. Because they are both big campuses in great cities, Juan knows that he will be happy at either school.

Applying to colleges with the right combination of early admissions policies helps Juan minimize his stress and maximize his chances of getting into his dream school. All students should understand the benefits of early decision, early action, and other types of early admissions programs. Chapter 6, Making the Most of Early Admissions Policies, gives you all the information you need to make the right decision about applying early.

PATH #4: THE SIZEIST

As the name implies, *sizeists* are students who emphasize the size of the school in their college search. Sizeists know that they learn best in a particular type of classroom. Do you learn more and get better grades in classes where you have a relationship with your teacher? Do you respond to teachers who are more involved in giving you feedback? Do you find class discussion especially rewarding? If you answered yes to any of these questions, you might benefit from a small college that promotes seminar-style classes taught by professors. Do you learn more from reading the textbook on your own than you do from being in the classroom? Do you hate talking in class or think that group discussions can be a waste of time? If you answered yes to any of these questions, you might prefer a large university with lectures that encourage students to be independent learners.

Carrie, a student at a public school outside of San Diego, is a classic sizeist. Growing up as the third of five girls in a traditional Irish-Catholic family, Carrie has always been described as the sensitive one in her family, a title that she earned from years of deep attachment to parents, siblings, babysitters, and friends. Naturally, Carrie's emphasis on her relationships extends to her life at school. Though the most common letter on her Poway High School transcript is a B+, the upper and lower range of her grades can generally be explained by her feelings about the teacher. That A in tenth-grade World History? Dr. Van Wie was the best teacher ever—incredibly kind, unusually fashionable, and she could draw a perfect map of medieval Europe on the blackboard freehand. The D in Marching Band freshman year? Mr. Demetrio caught her texting her friend Natalie and had it in for her. Carrie figured that there was no point in going to that class since Mr. Demetrio already hated her and probably wouldn't notice since there were so many students in the band.

When it comes to college, there are only four letters that Carrie knows: UCSD (University of California at San Diego). Both her parents are alumni, and her two older sisters, who still come home every week for the family Sunday dinner, are currently enrolled there. When the dinner table discussion turns to the topic of college in the winter of Carrie's junior year, she is surprised when her sisters suggest she look at some smaller schools. For the first time, Carrie considers that she might be happier at a college where she can get to know her professors and get involved in class discussions.

Later that week, Carrie uses the College Board website to search for small liberal arts colleges within five hundred miles of zip code 92064. She eliminates some of the fifty or so results based on selectivity and ends up with a list of schools with names that sound at least somewhat familiar: Chapman, Whittier, Occidental, Loyola Marymount, Concordia, Pepperdine, and San Diego Christian College.

A few weeks later, Carrie and her mother set out on their college visits. At Pepperdine, Carrie's tour guide talks about the wonderful dinner invitations that faculty members regularly extend. At Occidental, Carrie sits in on a psychology class with just six students and the professor where everyone calls each other by first name. The only school she doesn't like is San Diego Christian College because it is *too* small—fewer than five hundred students total.

Carrie ultimately decides that Pepperdine is her first choice, both for its intimate campus atmosphere and its Christian affiliation. Since Pepperdine doesn't have an early decision or early action program, Carrie decides to apply to seven schools regular decision: Pepperdine, Occidental, Chapman, Whittier, Loyola Marymount, Concordia, and, of course, UCSD, which she keeps on her list just in case.

Sizeists like Carrie benefit most from campus visits that allow them to get a sense of the academic experience at different colleges. Though it is not always possible to visit every school on your college list, sizeists should make a point of visiting campuses while classes are in session instead of in the summer or during holidays. In chapter 3, Getting a Good Gut Feeling, I provide lots of tips for campus visits.

PATH #5: THE CHILL PILL

There are many different reasons that students don't get perfect grades in high school. Some could probably be straight-A students if they really tried, but they have neither the drive nor the discipline to get perfect grades in every course. Others struggle in certain subjects like math or English but do well in the classes they genuinely enjoy. And then there are the students who have to work hard and put in extra hours to get Bs. For whatever reason, good grades just don't come easily to them. These students—I call them the *chill pills*—are better suited to colleges with less demanding, more supportive academic environments. When it comes to academic stress, less is more for them.

Elizabeth, a chill pill at a high school near Dallas, knows that she will do best at a college with a reasonable academic workload. School has always been a source of stress for Elizabeth. In third grade, she started to get painful headaches whenever she had an exam or report due. By middle school, her stress headaches were constant during midterms and finals. Over time, Elizabeth learned to cope with them. Now in high school, she is resolved to doing her best in school even if she rarely makes it to the top of her class.

In her junior year, Elizabeth takes a trip to Boston to visit her academic idol—her close friend and cousin, Alice, a freshman at MIT. Though they have always been close, Alice and Elizabeth are very different kinds of students. In high school, Alice earned perfect grades and SAT scores, won all kinds of awards for math and science, and was captain of the varsity fencing team. Instead of feeling jealous of her cousin's seemingly effortless accomplishments, Elizabeth loves being Alice's biggest cheerleader.

When she gets to MIT, Elizabeth is surprised by how much pressure Alice is under. She spends most of the weekend studying, and Elizabeth is forced to tour Boston by herself. Figuring that she might as well be productive, Elizabeth heads over to Boston University for a campus tour. It would be fun to go to a college close to Alice— assuming she ever stops studying.

Elizabeth makes it to the BU Admissions Office just in time to grab one of the last seats at the "Meet Boston University" information session. There, she learns about Boston University's College of

General Studies (CGS), a supportive two-year program in liberal arts where professors teach seminar-like classes and provide a nurturing environment. After two years, CGS students transfer to one of BU's undergraduate colleges where they pursue the courses required for their major and graduate with a bachelor's degree.

Elizabeth decides to head over to CGS to see for herself. Before she gets too far, she is greeted by a familiar voice belonging to Brian, a family friend from Texas. Elizabeth and Brian spend the next two hours walking around campus and catching up. By the time he gets around to describing the CGS workload—"Not a piece of cake but easier than high school in a lot of ways because you have less time in class and more time to study"—Elizabeth is sold on the College of General Studies program at BU. She especially likes the little touches that indicate a supportive environment, like how CGS does not allow midterms and finals from different classes to be scheduled on the same day. Elizabeth decides that she is going to use CGS as a yardstick with which to compare other schools. This is a program where she can get a good education without killing herself to survive academically.

Because colleges don't necessarily measure or advertise how much stress their students are under, chill pills like Elizabeth need to do their homework to find the right school. The best resources for chill pills are current students who can give them the real scoop on their academic experiences. Unlike tour guides whose job it is to represent the university in a positive light, students like Elizabeth's friend Brian are happy to give her a more balanced perspective. If you don't know anyone at a particular college, statistics like transfer rates and percentages of students on academic probation may provide some insight into the overall level of academic difficulty at the school. Chapter 2, Building a College List, breaks down the various sources of information that students can use to get the scoop on different campuses.

PATH #6: THE BARGAIN HUNTER

With skyrocketing tuition price tags and unprecedented levels of student debt, you don't have to be living below the poverty line to be concerned about college costs. Maybe you're a hardworking, middle-class student who doesn't want to graduate with mortgage-sized student loans before you've even gone on your first job interview. Maybe you know that you want to go to graduate school and would like your education budget to stretch beyond the four years it takes to get a bachelor's degree. Maybe you are a millionaire who would prefer a college that offers a good education at a reasonable price. Whatever the circumstances, students who put cost at the top of their college search criteria can be considered *bargain hunters*.

When it comes to college, Jack, a middle-class student in Queens, New York, is looking for the most affordable option. As the oldest of three children living with their single mother, Jack grew up doing lots of little things to save or earn money—he gets books from the library, brings lunch to school, and is the go-to snow shoveler in his neighborhood. Jack's frugality paid off when he was able to buy himself a reliable used car with savings from his after-school job at Fun Zone, the children's party center where he was recently promoted to shift manager.

One night toward the end of his sophomore year, Jack and his mother talk seriously for the first time about paying for college. Jack has always figured that he would get financial aid because his mother's income as a pediatric nurse isn't enough to cover the cost of college and raising three children in an expensive city like New York. However, Jack is disappointed to learn that his financial aid might be limited when colleges take his father's earnings into account—even though Jack's father lives in Memphis and has made it clear that his financial priorities lie elsewhere.

Before he applies to college, Jack decides to educate himself about the financial aid process. He attends a financial aid information session at the local library and consults his guidance counselor about his options. They come up with two lists. The first is filled with public schools that offer discounted tuition for in-state residents: four schools that belong to the State University of New York (SUNY) system—Binghamton, Albany, Stonybrook, and Purchase—and three City University of New York (CUNY) schools—Hunter, Queens, and Brooklyn colleges. The second list is informed by a quick search on the College Board website that turns up 294 four-year colleges within two hundred miles of his hometown that offer merit scholarships. Jack narrows down the list to six schools—St. Joseph's College, Manhattanville College,

Marist College, Adelphi University, College of New Rochelle, and St. Johns University—based on his guidance counselor's knowledge of where students from his high school with similar GPAs have gotten merit scholarships in the past.

Jack leaves the meeting feeling empowered. He starts working on the itinerary for his college visits over the summer. As a bargain hunter, Jack doesn't want to get too attached to a particular school early on because he knows that he won't be able to compare the actual cost of attendance at the colleges on his list until he applies for aid and gets his financial aid award letters. Chapter 11, Paying for College, outlines everything bargain hunters need to know about the different types of financial aid for college.

CHOOSING YOUR OWN ADVENTURE

Amy, Julia, Juan, Carrie, Elizabeth, and Jack had very different approaches to finding colleges that would fit their needs. However, these students share one important thing in common: they recognized their priorities early and conducted a focused college search. Some of you will immediately identify with one of these students, while others will recognize parts of yourselves in a few of these stories. If you love the idea of joining a fraternity in college, but you also want to go to a school where you can get to know your professors, you might be an atmospherist *and* a sizeist. If prestige is your thing but you don't want to work too hard, you probably identify with the brand-name shopper *and* the chill pill. If you prioritize affordability and you know exactly what you want to study, you can relate to both the bargain hunter *and* the special agent.

But what if you have absolutely no idea what you want to study or what type of campus best suits you? You are not the only teenager out there who is confused about the future. The next chapter will walk you through the process of how to identify your college priorities and start to put together a list of schools that meet your needs.

CHAPTER 2

BUILDING A COLLEGE LIST

Generations of scholars and experts have taught us that good decision making is rooted in facts and reason. Our society puts so much emphasis on the superiority of rational thought that we often refer to rational thinking as *the* thing that separates humans from animals. However, psychologists and neuroscientists who study the human brain have discovered that we use both reason and emotions in good decision making, whether we're choosing a new shirt or a new car. Reason helps us to narrow down our options (price, style, color, and so on), and our emotions guide us in making the ultimate selection; when choosing from different options, we'll usually buy the shirt that makes us feel happiest in the dressing room or avoid the used car whose rattle makes us feel anxious during the test drive. The best decisions are made up of two equally important parts: (1) thoughtfully considered, objective facts and (2) an honest assessment of how something makes us feel.

Ignoring either of these components can lead to decisions that we come to regret.

Choosing the right college is similar to any other important decision you will make in your life—you need to consider both the objective qualities of the college and how you feel when you visit the campus. Once you start talking to real college students about how they chose their particular school, you'll meet plenty of disappointed people who ignored their emotions ("The only reason I came here was because it was the best school I got into") or didn't take important facts into account ("I regret coming here because this school is just too expensive"). You'll also come across lots of happy college students who will tell you how they made the right choice for them using both rational and emotional reasons ("I looked at this school because it had my major, but the minute I stepped onto the campus it just felt right"). This chapter and the next show you how to be one of the happy college students, using both reason and emotion to choose a school that will allow you to thrive as a student and a person.

IDENTIFYING YOUR PRIORITIES

The first step in putting together a college list is to be honest with yourself and reflect on what you want and what you don't want from a college. There are many factors to consider. Answering the following questions will help you understand more about what is important to you and what you need to succeed in the next stage of your life. Once you know more about your preferences, you can start narrowing down the list of schools that might fit your criteria.

LOCATION/CAMPUS SETTING
- How far do you want to be from home?
- Do you want to be in a city, the country, or a suburb?
- Is it important to you that the college has good "town-gown relations"—that is, a good rapport with the community that surrounds it?

SCHOOL TYPE

- Do you prefer a liberal arts college that focuses on undergraduate education, a research university that also has graduate schools, or a technical school that specializes in preprofessional majors like engineering or graphic design?
- Is it important to you that professors—not teaching assistants or graduate students—teach all your classes?
- Do you care about having access to faculty outside of class?
- Would you be happy at a school that targets a specific demography like a women's college, a Catholic college, or an HBCU (historically black college/university)?

SCHOOL SIZE

- Would you prefer a small college (under three thousand students), a medium-sized school (three to eight thousand students), or a large university (eight thousand plus students)?

MAJORS/MINORS

- Do you have strong preferences for majors and/or minors? If so, here are some things to consider about particular colleges on your list:
  - › Does the college offer the major that you want?
  - › Do you have the option of choosing a minor in addition to your major?
  - › Can you double-major, if you have two strong areas of interest?
  - › Can you create your own customized major from courses in different departments? (For example, if you are interested in theatrical set design, can you combine courses from the drama and art departments to create an individualized major in set design?)
  - › Do students who major in certain subjects take longer to graduate than others?

COLLEGE COURSE REQUIREMENTS

- Do you want to be at a college with an open curriculum that will allow you to take whatever classes you want, a college with rigid course requirements that will ensure you will graduate with certain skills such as learning a foreign language, or something in between? .

COLLEGE COSTS AND FINANCIAL AID

- Do you need financial aid for college? If so, here are some questions to ask about the specific colleges on your list:
  - › What is the cost of tuition, fees, room, board, and books?
  - › What percentage of students at the college receives financial aid?
  - › What percentage of financial need does the college commit to meeting?
  - › Can the financial aid package be adjusted if there is a change in your family's circumstances, such as the loss of a job or if a sibling is also in college?
  - › Is work-study available and easy to get? (For more on work-study, see "The Anatomy of a Financial Aid Award Letter" on page 176.)
  - › Does the college offer any need-based grants or scholarships to students? What are the criteria? Are these awards renewable?

DIVERSITY/CAMPUS CULTURE

- Do you care about the male-female ratio of students on campus?
- Do you want to go to a college where both women and men take on leadership positions?
- Is it important for you to have racial/ethnic/religious diversity on campus?
- Is it important to be able to practice your religion on campus? Do you want to have access to a church, mosque, synagogue, or temple?
- Do you want to be in the racial/ethnic/religious/gender majority on campus?

- Do you want a college with a strong LGBT community?
- Do you prefer to go to school with other students from your hometown/state/country?

SOCIAL LIFE

- Do you want to join a fraternity or sorority?
- If you do not want to be part of a fraternity or sorority, do you mind going to a college that has Greek life?
- Do you plan to drink in college, or do you prefer a school that hosts lots of "dry" campus parties and events?
- Do you want a college with good athletic teams and strong attendance at athletic events?
- Do you want a school that emphasizes community service?
- Are there particular extracurricular organizations—school newspaper, debate clubs, campus radio station, or others—that you would like to join in college?
- Is it important for you to go to a college with strong "school spirit"? If so, ask:
  › Are there many campus traditions?
  › Does everyone know and sing the school song?
  › What is the alumni giving rate? (This is the percentage of graduates who donate money to the school; it can be a good indicator of alumni satisfaction.)

POLITICS

- Do you want a "political" campus? If so, do you care if most of the students agree with your point of view or are you open to being in the political minority?

ACADEMIC SUPPORT/GRADING POLICIES

- Do you need any special academic support services to help you succeed academically? (If you have been diagnosed with a learning disability, see chapter 10, Communicating Your Experience.)
- Do you want a college that will allow you to take courses pass/fail?

- Is it important to you to be able to get into your first-choice courses each semester?
- Do you want a college that has flexible policies for adding or dropping courses?
- Do you plan on studying abroad?

GRADUATION RATES
- Is it important to you to graduate within four years?

POSTGRADUATION SUPPORT
- Do you hope to get a job right after college? If so:
  › What are the career advising resources?
  › Can you get help with resume and interview preparation?
  › What percentage of students get jobs immediately after graduation?
  › What is the placement rate for students who look for jobs immediately after graduation?
  › Are there any ongoing professional networking opportunities for alumni?
  › Do alumni have access to the college's career advising services?
- Are you considering a certain preprofessional path that will require you to eventually earn a graduate degree? If so:
  › What kind of advising is available for graduate school?
  › What percentage of students go on to graduate school?
  › What percentage of students who apply to graduate school are accepted?
  › Does the university have graduate programs that you might be interested in? Do they give preferential treatment to undergraduates from their institution?
- Is it important for you to have an internship while in college? If so, ask:
  › What kind of resources are available to help students find internships?
  › What percentage of students has internships while enrolled in school?
  › Can students get course credit for internships?

Take a minute to look over your answers to these questions. Can you spot any themes? Are there certain things—location, size, Greek life, politics, graduation rate—that seem nonnegotiable? If so, take a moment to write down your priorities.

Now look over your list and circle the three things that are most important to you. These are your major priorities—the things that you absolutely need to consider, such as cost or whether the college offers the courses you want to take. The rest of the list constitutes your minor priorities—the things that you'd like to have, such as good sports teams or Greek life.

Making a priority list is the first step in finding your Dream U. This is the rational part of the process where you use your preferences about things like size, location, and graduate school placement to put together a manageable list of schools that you will later visit. (See chapter 3, Getting a Good Gut Feeling, for more information on campus visits.) Your college list should only include schools that fit each of your three major priorities and at least some of your minor priorities.

SEARCH ENGINE DATABASES

As a high school student of the twenty-first century, you don't even have to leave your house to figure out whether or not particular colleges meet the criteria on your priorities list. There are two types of online resources that can help you narrow down your college list: search engine databases and online reviews. *Search engine databases* are websites that let you input your priorities—things like location, size, price, acceptance rates, average SAT scores, student-faculty ratio, and other factors. They then comb through data on thousands of colleges and generate a list that fits your broad criteria. Don't be afraid if the database comes back with a bunch of schools you've never heard of before. That's why you're doing this research; there are literally thousands of colleges out there, and you are trying to learn more about your options.

You can also use search engine databases to get basic information about schools that people recommended but that you don't know much about—like the college your cousin loves or the school your English teacher thinks would be perfect for you. Search engine databases can tell you important things about a school, including acceptance rates, standardized test averages, whether they have your intended major, and how much they charge for tuition and fees. If the college fits all of your major priorities and most of your minor priorities, you can add it to your list.

You need to use reputable search engine database websites to get reliable data. I recommend the College Search option on the College Board website (https://bigfuture.collegeboard.org) and the College Navigator from the National Center for Education Statistics run by the U.S. Department of Education (http://nces.ed.gov/collegenavigator). Both websites give you many categories to choose from and allow you to use your own search criteria so that you can consider colleges that meet your preferences for location, size, and majors. If you care a lot about certain intangibles—for example, you only want "preppy," "LGBT friendly" schools in "great college towns"—you might want to check out the Super Match search engine on the College Confidential website (www.collegeconfidential.com). These criteria are subjective, but Super Match can give you some ideas for colleges that may appeal to you. It will also give you results that don't meet 100 percent of your search criteria (and explain how these colleges meet most, but not all, of your priorities) so you won't have to rule out schools that have most of the things you are looking for. Finally, if cost is on your list of major priorities, the Department of Education also hosts the College Affordability and Transparency Center (http://collegecost.ed.gov/catc). This site is a great source of information for bargain hunters because you can find a list of the most affordable colleges as well as estimate the *net costs* (the cost of attendance after scholarships and grants) at particular schools.

STUDENT REVIEWS

Once you have poked around the search engine databases and generated a college list based on your basic priorities, reading reviews and comments from actual students can help you get a sense of the culture of the school. *The Princeton Review's 377 Best Colleges* is one of my favorite guidebooks because the information is based on over 100,000 different student reviews. This book is great for getting the student point of view on some of the colleges that you found from search engine databases. You can also learn about other colleges that might interest you by looking at their rankings pages, especially for nontraditional categories like "Students Pack the Stadiums" and "Dorms Like Palaces." I suggest keeping this book in a place where you can browse through it at your leisure—the bathroom, next to your bed, in the car (as long as you are not driving!). The best thing to do is to cover up the name of the school at the top of the page and just read descriptions of different colleges and what the students have to say. That way you limit any bias you might associate with a particular campus.

You can find several online resources for student reviews of colleges, but I find that College Prowler (www.collegeprowler.com) is the easiest to read and navigate. College Prowler allows you to scroll through hundreds of students' comments about what life on campus is really like. Because these reviews are unfiltered, be prepared to read a lot about things like the dining halls, on-campus parking, and whether the girls or guys are good-looking. These might not be the most important things to consider when compared to your major and minor priorities list, but it never hurts to hear what real students think about the "quality of life" things that search engines can't capture. College Confidential (www.collegeconfidential.com) is another popular site that offers students and parents the chance to share their experiences and impressions in an online community and discussions forum. Admissions experts also weigh in to offer accurate information and stop false rumors from spreading. A particularly interesting feature on College Confidential is the Campus Vibe section where students and parents can post videos from campus tours. You can learn a lot from other students who are struggling to find the information session on campus or prepping for an on-campus interview.

To be fair, you shouldn't base your entire impression of a college on books or websites that offer student reviews. These reviews can be misleading because they are not necessarily representative of all students on campus. Students with more extreme views—both positive and negative—may be more likely to leave a review on a website or fill out a form in the student center. Plus, these reviews are just opinions that you might not always agree with. Some of my favorite books or restaurants have received mixed online reviews. Don't completely eliminate a college that fits all your other major and minor priorities just because you read a couple of negative student reviews. It may still be worth visiting the campus so that you can form an impression with your own two eyes.

COLLEGE RANKINGS

It may be hard for students to believe this, but there was a time when even Ivy League schools were worried about getting quality students. After the baby boom in the 1950s, there was a dip in the nation's birth rate and there were fewer high school students in the late 1970s than there had been previously. Colleges began aggressively competing with each other over a smaller applicant pool. In 1983, the editors at a magazine called *U.S. News & World Report* realized that students needed a way to compare the colleges that were sending them piles of brochures. And so the college rankings were born.

Much controversy surrounds the *U.S. News* ranking methodology, which relies on variables like selectivity, average SAT scores, and alumni-giving rates. It's hard to argue that *U.S. News* actually measures the quality of education at the schools that they rank. However, students can use college rankings as one of several sources of information to help put together a college list. These rankings are most helpful in getting a sense of the prestige factor for the colleges that you are considering. Students who really care about prestige may want to rely on the rankings a little more heavily; those who do not may choose to ignore rankings entirely. No matter where you fall, just remember that these rankings are put together by editors who want to sell magazines. They are neither objective nor definitive measures of college quality.

APPROACHING STRANGERS IN SWEATSHIRTS AND OTHER OLD-FASHIONED WAYS TO GET INFORMATION

Picture this: You are waiting in line at the supermarket checkout with a few items that your mom asked you to pick up for dinner when you notice that the man in front of you is wearing a Denison University sweatshirt. Denison, a medium-sized liberal arts college near Columbus, Ohio, keeps coming up in your search engine lists. It meets all your priorities for size, intended major, cost, graduation rates, admissions criteria, and graduate school placement. But you know nothing about it and you don't know anyone who went there. As a savvy student, you decide to take advantage of your good fortune and introduce yourself to this Denison sweatshirt–clad stranger. It turns out that he just graduated and had a great experience. He answers all your questions and convinces you that you should go for a visit.

Although it's not very scientific, one of the best ways to get information about what life at a particular college is really like is to talk to actual students or graduates. So put on your networking hat! Even if you need to work up a little courage first, there's no shame in walking up to a stranger in the grocery store or bank who is wearing some college garb and just asking them about their experiences. You can also ask your teachers and guidance counselors if they know other students from your school who are enrolled in that college. Posting something like "Looking for students or graduates of Muhlenberg College" on Facebook may also lead to some contacts and interesting conversations. Don't be afraid to get creative, and keep your eyes peeled for good information.

CAN I GET IN?

Once you find the colleges that fit your priorities list, an important question still remains: can I get in? Because the admissions process has many subjective components, it's impossible to answer this question with data alone; you'll never know for sure until you apply. However, there is a fantastic new tool called Naviance that can help you assess your chances by comparing yourself to similar applicants from the past. Naviance is a subscription-based service to which school districts across the country subscribe. Your school enters basic information about other students (GPA and standardized test scores) who went to your high school during the past three years, along with where they applied to college and whether or not they were accepted. Naviance lets you compare your basic academic credentials with those of your peers to see if you are at, above, or below the average GPA and standardized test scores for a particular college. The database does not provide data on whether or not individual students from your high school had admissions "hooks" like athletics or legacy status, but you can view the data in graph form to look for outliers that might skew the averages.

PUTTING TOGETHER A COLLEGE LIST

I don't believe that the perfect college list has a fixed number of colleges. Some students have really specific preferences and will easily narrow down their list to a few schools. Others will find that they want to cast a wider net because they need to compare financial aid offers (see chapter 11) or because they want to include several very selective schools. Instead of focusing on a specific number of colleges, students with less-than-perfect academic records should be sure to have a balance of different types of schools on their list.

- **Safety schools** are colleges that definitely should accept you. Colleges that accept more than 50 percent of applicants are pretty safe bets for B students or better—just make sure that your standardized tests are at least in the fiftieth percentile for admitted students. Because the process can be a little unpredictable, it's a good idea for all students to have at least two safety schools. As I explain in chapter 11, Paying for College, students applying for financial aid at schools that are "need aware" (i.e., colleges that consider whether or not a student needs financial aid when making their admissions decisions) might want a few more.

- **Target schools** are colleges that generally accept students with your academic credentials. These colleges are still selective (they accept between 35 and 50 percent of applicants), but students whose test scores match their averages should have a good shot.

- **Reach schools** are colleges that generally accept students with better academic credentials. Consider very selective colleges—those that accept between 25 and 35 percent of applicants—as reach schools as long as your test scores are in the range for admitted students. If you fall in love with a reach school and follow all the advice in this book, your best shot of getting in is to apply early (see chapter 6, Making the Most of Early Admissions Policies).

CHAPTER 2 ACTION STEPS

❏ Make a priorities list by answering the questions in this chapter.

❏ Use your priorities list to put together your college list. Good sources of information include search engine databases, student reviews, college rankings lists, and good old-fashioned conversations with students and alumni.

❏ Use your knowledge of what makes a particular college selective to assess your chances of getting in.

❏ Put together a college list that has a combination of reach, target, and safety schools. Make sure that every single college on this list meets your major priorities and most of your minor priorities.

CHAPTER 3

GETTING A GOOD GUT FEELING

I am always surprised when I meet students who have enrolled at a college that they never visited before they set foot on campus for orientation. Of course, I understand that traveling to colleges can be expensive, and not everyone has the resources to tour every school that might be a good match. Even so, college is probably the biggest financial investment you'll make aside from buying a house—and you would never buy a house sight unseen, right?

As a student without a perfect high school transcript, it is especially important that you know what you are "buying" when it comes to college. Unlike your valedictorian peers, you are probably a little pickier when it comes to your learning environment—you might favor certain subjects, teachers, and classroom atmospheres over others. The first two chapters of this book focused on helping you understand yourself better so that you can select a college that will allow you to thrive. Once you know what you're looking for, it will be easier to identify the right fit for you when you see it.

One of the most frequently asked questions I get is this: when should I start looking at colleges? The truth is that it is never too early to get a sense of what is out there. There is merit in just walking around a local campus to get a taste of college life in early high school. However, you probably won't be ready to look at colleges to which you might seriously consider applying until the second half of your sophomore year or the first semester of junior year. Until then, you're still discovering what kind of student you are, which environments are best suited to your learning style, and which subjects you enjoy in school. You'll also have very little information about your standardized testing abilities before you take the PSATs, so it can be hard to determine which colleges might be good academic matches.

Do you have to visit every college that you apply to before you send in your application? Of course not. You can always visit some of the colleges on your list after you are accepted. In fact, many schools will even cover travel costs for accepted students, especially those who qualify for financial aid. (You can call the admissions office and inquire about travel subsidies once you get in.) If you have a long list of colleges and can't make it to all of them, I suggest that you focus on visiting the more selective schools on your list—your reach and target schools—and save your safeties for later.

WHY VISIT?

It is important to visit the more selective colleges on your list for two reasons. Chapter 6 explains the advantages of early decision and early action programs in more detail, but for now, it is important to understand that your best chance of getting into your reach school is to apply early. The problem is that early decision programs are binding, which means that you must enroll at the college if accepted. Therefore, you'll have to visit all the schools to which you might want to apply early decision. Otherwise, it's sort of like buying an airline ticket on Priceline—you'd better make sure that you want to take that trip before you bid because you will have to get on the plane if they accept your offer. You want to be certain that your early decision school is your absolute first choice because you don't want to have any regrets if you are accepted.

Another reason to visit the more selective colleges on your list is because admissions officers often track a student's interest in their school. There are two very important statistics in college admissions—acceptance rates and yield. The *acceptance rate* is pretty self-explanatory: it's the percentage of applicants that the college admits. This statistic is easily accessible in most college guidebooks. The *yield* is the percentage of accepted students who actually enroll. This number is much harder to find but no less important because colleges with low yields have to accept more students. No college wants to be thought of as everybody's safety school. When choosing between two qualified students, most admissions officers are more likely to select the one who seems more excited about the school and, therefore, more likely to enroll. As a B student, one of the things you can do to boost your chances of admission to the more selective colleges on your list is to demonstrate your enthusiasm for these schools. The first step in doing so is to visit the campus—and don't forget to sign in at the admissions office so they have a record of your visit!

TIMING

The best time to visit a college is when classes are in session. You don't just want to look at the library, cafeteria, and gym; you want to see what the students and professors are like and get a sense of whether or not you'd be happy there. Even though you may be visiting with your family, take some time to walk around the campus by yourself. Discretely listen in on students' conversations in the cafeteria. Look at the expressions on their faces as they hurry past you on the quad. Go to the student center and browse the bulletin board to see what's happening that weekend. Sit in on a class and observe the discussion. Picture yourself at this school in a year or two and imagine what you might do there—and more importantly ask yourself: *how will going to this college help me grow as a person?*

TAKE NOTES

The best piece of advice I can give you is to *take notes* while you are on campus (a voice recorder on your smartphone can serve this purpose as well as a pen and notepad). There are two reasons why it is important to record your impressions and the details that make each school distinct. First, you'll likely be visiting a lot of colleges before this process is finished, and many students find that the campuses, tours, and information sessions start to blend together. As you narrow down your list, it is incredibly useful to review your notes and remember the enthusiasm you felt when you saw the new science labs or the terror that overcame you when you heard about that brutal foreign language requirement. These are the details that might help you decide among schools a few months down the line when your memory is fuzzy and the brochures all start to look the same.

The second reason that it is so important to take notes is that there are numerous points in the application process when colleges ask applicants a basic question: why do you want to go to school here? You should be prepared to answer this question in supplementary essays, during your college interview, when you meet with your guidance counselor, and in any correspondence you have with the admissions office. This question looks easy on the surface, but it trips up many students, those who rely on generic, unimpressive answers like "the beautiful campus" or "the great location" or—my least favorite—"because it's a great school." Many colleges will fit these descriptions; you need to go into much more detail to capture a college's unique qualities and show the admissions committee how you can take advantage of what they have to offer and make a contribution to the community. If you have good notes, you'll be in better shape than your unprepared A student rivals.

QUESTIONS TO GUIDE YOUR NOTE TAKING
- What are three things that stand out about the school? (These are three things that should apply to this school *only*—instead of "great museum," think "the accessibility of the Spencer Museum's world-renowned art collection, which includes

everything from Winslow Homer's landscapes to masterpieces from the Japanese Edo period.")

- What are some of the unique academic offerings of this college? (Again, don't be generic or use descriptions that can apply to other colleges—instead of "small classes," write "the impressive student theater at the Barrett Center is open to five student-run productions each year.")
- How are these programs or opportunities aligned with your academic interests?
- Name a tradition or value that is emphasized by the school that seems unique to you. How does this tradition or value connect to you as a person?
- List three adjectives that you heard repeated by different people on campus when they described the school. Why do these qualities appeal to you?
- How can you make a unique contribution to the school? (Be specific: "I hope to compose music and sing alto for the award-winning campus a cappella group, the Aca Belles; I want to conduct research on electric currents through the Women in Engineering program and present at the annual student symposium.")
- If you were a student at this school, how do you think you would spend a free afternoon taking advantage of the resources on campus? (Again, be specific: "I would start by spending a few hours in the Hampton Pottery Studio, attend a race relations book club meeting of the African-American Student Association, try some adventurous locavore dishes at the innovative Bartley Dining Hall, and finish up with a Fellini movie at the Smith Theater.")

SEEK OUT STUDENTS

When visiting college campuses, many students make plans to take the campus tour or sit in on an information session sponsored by the admissions office. These activities can be helpful, but the best way to measure student satisfaction on campus is to *talk to actual students*. Ideally, it would be great to have lunch with a student on campus during your visit. Check your Facebook friends to see if you know anyone there—most students are happy to entertain prospective freshmen. If you don't know any current students, there are easy ways to meet some. One great option is to look up a contact name for a club or team that you might like to join—the school newspaper, marching band, Young Democrats/Republicans, or some other group that interests you. Many schools will have contacts for these organizations listed on their websites, or you can call the admissions office to point you in the right direction. When you find a group that looks interesting, email the student representative and ask if you might be able to get together for coffee when you're on campus. If you can't locate this information, you can always just find a friendly face in the cafeteria and strike up a conversation. You'll be surprised by how friendly—and honest!—most college students are.

QUESTIONS TO ASK CURRENT STUDENTS

- Does the school have a good freshman orientation program? How long did it take for you to feel at home here?
- Is it easy to register for classes? Do the most popular classes fill up quickly?
- What kind of dorm room did you have as a first-year student? How many roommates did you have?
- Did you have any trouble covering your college costs? Did your financial aid package change at all from year to year? Were you able to talk to someone in the financial aid office if you had a problem?
- How big is your biggest class? How small is your smallest class?
- How often do you talk to your professors?
- Have you used the campus career center? What did you think of the support you got?
- Do you have an adviser? Is your adviser helpful?
- Is it hard to find a work-study job if you want one?
- What is your typical weekend like?
- How many hours a day do you spend studying?
- Is there anything you would change about the school?

- If you could go back in time to your senior year of high school, is there anything you know now about this school that you wish you had known then?
- What are some common mistakes you see students at this college make?

THE CAMPUS TOUR

If you don't have a friend who can show you around campus, it is worthwhile to take the admissions office tour during your visit. Every college offers campus tours, usually given by enthusiastic undergraduates who are paid work-study wages for their time. The best thing about taking a tour is that is gives you the opportunity to get a general sense of the layout of the campus. Be sure to take notes on some of the things that impress you, using details like the names of buildings you'd spend time in if you were a student at this college or the specific campus traditions that stand out to you. This is also a good opportunity to investigate the logistical aspects of student life. Are the freshman dorms a twenty-minute walk from the gym where you would like to work out in the mornings? If the campus is big, is it easy to get around by bus or bike? Can you have a car if you want one? Where are the nearest bookstores, grocery stores, banks, and drugstores?

Once you start visiting a few different campuses, you will be surprised by how similar the tour guide scripts start to sound. Colleges tend to promise students a lot of the same things: personal attention, excellent facilities, flexible curricula, outstanding job and graduate school placement, fun campus traditions, gourmet food, and palatial dorm rooms. Going back to our going-to-college-is-the-financial-equivalent-of-buying-a-house analogy, you can think of your tour guides as realtors. They highlight the best parts of the school and gloss over the worst because the goal is to get you to "buy" the college. It's not that college tour guides are *lying*; they just have a lens through which they are filtering information. As a savvy high school student, your job is to interpret what you hear on your college tour with an understanding that the tour guide's job is to make the college look as attractive as possible.

Whatever happens on your campus tour, *don't judge a college by the tour guide*. I can't tell you how many students inform me that they liked or did not like a particular college because of how they felt about the tour guide. It would be pretty silly to choose a college that didn't have the major you are interested in just because the tour guide was good-looking, smart, and interesting. By the same token, you also don't want to overlook a school that might be a perfect academic match just because you thought your tour guide was an obnoxious bore. Students on college campuses are not like the Borg on *Star Trek*—they don't all share the same brain. It is important to use the campus tour as one of many pieces of information that you get about a college.

QUESTIONS TO ASK YOUR TOUR GUIDE

- When viewing a sample dorm room: Would I have a room like this as a freshman?
- What is your *least favorite* building on campus?
- Is there a student stereotype here and, if so, in what ways would you say that it's accurate—or not?
- Does the college operate a student shuttle and, if so, where does it go (for example, around the campus, to nearby colleges, downtown, malls, airport, bus station, or other locations)? How often and how late does it run?
- What are some of the places that students from this college tend to congregate *off* campus? Are there places in this town (or city) where students from more than one college tend to hang out together?
- Do dorms close during major vacations? If so, can students stay somewhere on campus if home is far away?
- Roughly what percentage of students stays on campus on the weekends? (*Note:* This question is most appropriate if you are applying to public colleges out of state or looking at a college that seems to attract a lot of students from the local area.)
- How late is this library open? Is it open on weekends?
- What percentage of students receives financial aid on campus?
- What percentage of classes is taught by teaching assistants?
- What percentage of students studies abroad?

- Is it easy to register for classes?
- Is it easy to change your major, double-major, or design your own major?
- Can you tell me more about the academic support services on campus? How can I access a tutor, if I am having trouble in a class?
- How do students get around campus? Are freshmen allowed to have cars?
- What resources are available to students who want to get internships or jobs?
- Can you give me an example of a campus tradition that really illustrates the spirit of this college?
- Is it possible to sit in on a class while I'm here? (If so, take the opportunity!)
- What is the worst thing about being a student at this college?

INFORMATION SESSIONS

In addition to the campus tour, most colleges also host daily information sessions where an admissions officer (and sometimes a student) gives some general information about the school and answers questions about the admissions process (smaller colleges who don't have daily information sessions often offer one-on-one meetings with an admissions officer). These sessions usually last for about an hour and are generally held in the admissions office or nearby. (You can find schedules on the web or by calling the admissions office in advance.) The quality of these sessions varies a great deal. I've seen some admissions officers who are pretty forthright and try to give students some application tips, and others who dodge difficult questions and gloss over anything that might dissuade a student from applying. If you do attend an information session, focus on questions about *admissions* and *financial aid*. You can always get the scoop on the academic and social life from real students, but you won't always have access to someone who reads applications and makes admissions decisions.

QUESTIONS TO ASK DURING THE INFORMATION SESSION

Note: Considering that there will probably be many families in the audience, it's okay if you don't get to ask more than one or two of these.

QUESTIONS ABOUT THE ADMISSIONS PROCESS

- What are the acceptance rates for students who apply early decision versus students who apply regular decision?
- When you make a final decision on an applicant, are you aware of which other students have applied from the same high school? And, if so, how does that affect the verdicts?
- How important is GPA or class rank in admissions decisions?
- How important are extracurricular activities? Are there certain activities that you like to see more than others?
- How do you look at students who have part-time jobs?
- Do you consider whether a student is applying for financial aid when you make your admissions decisions?
- In your opinion, what makes a good college essay?
- How many letters of recommendation are required? Who should I ask to write on my behalf? Can I send additional letters of recommendation?
- Do you look at art or music supplements? Are they sent to faculty to be reviewed? How are they considered in the admissions process?
- What does your ideal applicant look like?
- What are some common mistakes that you see students make on their applications?
- Do you have any samples of applications or essays that you really liked?

QUESTIONS ABOUT HIGH SCHOOL COURSE WORK

- Are there particular courses that you want to see on a high school transcript?
- What happens if someone doesn't take the recommended courses in high school? If a student follows a passion for

ceramics and can't take physics, should he explain it in the additional information section?

- How do you factor in the rigor of courses when you look at a high school transcript?
- Would you rather see a community college class or an AP class at the high school on a high school transcript?
- Can summer academic course work "make up" for weaker academic performance during the year?

QUESTIONS ABOUT STANDARDIZED TEST SCORES

- What standardized tests are required for admissions? Does it help to take more tests than those that are required?
- How are standardized tests factored into admissions decisions?
- If I get better SAT or ACT test scores a couple weeks after the application deadline, will you still consider them if my school counselor faxes them to you promptly, even though the deadline has passed?
- I've been told that you use each applicant's best scores in each area, even if they come from different test dates. But do you still see all of the standardized test scores? If so, do you ever penalize a student for taking too many tests?

QUESTIONS ABOUT COLLEGE COURSE WORK

- Can nonmajors take classes in all other departments? If not, which departments are toughest for nonmajors to take classes in?
- I don't know what I want to major in. Will applying as "undecided" hurt me? How does applying as "undecided" make the admissions process different for me when compared to candidates who have already indicated their future major on the application?

YOUR REGIONAL
ADMISSIONS OFFICER

While you are already in the admissions office to attend the information session, it is a great idea to try to find out the *name* of your regional admissions officer, or the person who will be reading your application when you apply. I know this might sound intimidating, but as a student who wants to maximize your chances of acceptance, you should try to have some personal contact with the person who will be deciding your fate. College applications are not read at random; admissions officers are assigned to certain geographical regions. They travel to these places, visit the high schools, meet with local alumni, and are responsible for reading applications from students who live there. For example, when I worked at Dartmouth, my region included Long Island, Kansas, Missouri, Indiana, Maine, New Hampshire, Vermont, South America, Africa, India, and the Caribbean. If you lived in one of these areas and a representative from Dartmouth visited your high school when I worked there, chances are that I was both the person making this trip and the first one reading your application.

It's pretty easy to find out your regional admissions officer's name. Just walk into the reception area of the admissions office at any college and ask. Most reception desks keep business cards of all the admissions officers on file and are happy to give them out. Once you have this contact information, it's always nice to send an email to your regional admissions officer saying that you got her name on your campus visit and are looking forward to applying to this school. Ask if she will be visiting your high school or staffing a college fair in your area this year. (*Note:* The most popular time for admissions officers to do individual high school visits is late September through early November, and they tend to do large college fairs in the spring.) Once you know when your regional admissions officer will visit your area, make a point of going to an information session or college fair to introduce yourself in person. This is the first step toward building a relationship with your regional admissions officer, which may help you stand out in the applicant pool.

Part of an admissions officer's job is to travel to high schools and college fairs to meet with students and encourage them to apply. These weeks of travel are incredibly hectic—a typical day might include four high school visits, an early dinner with local alumni, and an information session in the evening. When they are on the road, admissions officers often find themselves answering the same questions again and again, eating bad fast food in their rental cars in between appointments, and spending too much time circling school parking lots looking for a spot. On a bad day, they might be greeted by a room full of disinterested blank stares or, even worse, they might fight traffic to get to a particular school only to find that no one has bothered to show up to their presentation. That's why it can be so nice for an admissions officer to see a friendly face in the audience and to meet students who are *genuinely* excited about their college. Most admissions officers will tell you that they have a special place in their hearts for a few students whom they meet on the road—and these students' applications get an especially close read.

It is worth your time to try to be one of these friendly faces. Try to track down the name of your regional admissions officer and find out her travel itinerary. If she is going to be in your area, make a point of going to the information session or college fair and introducing yourself. Keep in touch over email if you have any questions.

CHAPTER 3 ACTION STEPS

❏ Focus on visiting your reach and target schools first. You should see any school that you're thinking of applying to early and show interest while you're there.

❏ Try to visit campuses when classes are in session and talk to real students.

❏ When you are on campus, take notes so that you remember what made each college unique. Refer to them later when you write your college essay.

❏ Don't judge a college by the tour guide.

❏ Use information sessions to learn about admissions and financial aid.

❏ While you are on campus, find your regional admissions officer and introduce yourself, if you can.

CHAPTER 4

SELECTIVITY AND STANDARDIZED TESTING

Other countries have selective colleges that accept very few applicants, but the United States is the only country where the college admissions process is so confusing and unpredictable. In most parts of the world, students simply take one or several admissions exams. Those who score well are admitted to a particular university; those who do not are turned away. To be fair, because the stakes are so high, many students prepare ruthlessly and the competition can be fierce. At least the process is straightforward, however.

Spending time with American high school students and parents has taught me one thing over the years: most families are totally lost when it comes to understanding how the college admissions process works. And it's no wonder. Unlike universities in other countries that select students based solely on academic performance, American colleges also consider things like essays, recommendations, extracurricular activities, leadership, race/ethnicity/socioeconomic status, whether or not parents are alumni, and how far a student throws a football. American colleges try to please many different stakeholders through the admissions process: students, faculty, alumni, coaches, and the mighty college rankings. It's not just families that are confused about college admissions—the colleges themselves are trying to accomplish numerous goals when they select applicants.

WHY ARE COLLEGES SO SELECTIVE?

Students aren't the only ones competing against each other in the college admissions process. Selective colleges have the same type of rivalry, each one competing with its peer institutions over everything from recruiting desirable faculty to having the biggest endowment to building the best sports teams and facilities. Each of these factors raises a college's profile and has the potential to help make it more selective. Selective colleges are generally seen as more desirable by the people who fund them—their students and alumni. Selectivity is also a crucial component of the *U.S. News & World Report* rankings, which puts pressure on admissions offices to ensure that colleges continue to become more selective, even though many of them already turn away more students than they accept.

As I mentioned in chapter 3, a college's selectivity has two components: acceptance rates and yield. Universities go to great lengths to get as many applications as possible—they actively market themselves to prospective students and parents the same way that a company markets its products to consumers. Most colleges want you to apply even if you have no shot of getting in because every application they get helps make them more selective. Colleges also worry about their yield, or the number of accepted students who actually enroll. When a school has a low yield, they need to accept more students to fill their classes. This ultimately makes them less selective even if they get a ton of applications. That's why no college wants to be known as a "safety school."

How will you know if you have a chance of getting into a college if the admissions officer is likely going to encourage you to apply regardless? You'll need to look at a few statistics to figure out how selective the college really is. One of the most helpful numbers is the college's acceptance rate. (It's even better if you can get acceptance rates broken down for early and regular admission as well as in state and out of state, if appropriate.) Here are some categories to help you interpret acceptance rates:

- **Highly selective colleges:** These schools accept fewer than 25 percent of applicants; they turn away tons of A students, so students without a 4.0 should approach with caution, especially if they don't have a "hook" like being a recruited athlete or a legacy student.
- **Very selective colleges:** These schools accept between 25 and 35 percent of students; less-than-perfect students who follow the advice in this book might have a chance but should know that these colleges have more qualified, impressive applicants than they can accept. B students applying to very selective colleges need backups.
- **Selective colleges:** These schools accept between 35 and 50 percent of applicants; B students who put together good applications have a good shot at getting into these schools.
- **Safety schools:** These colleges accept the majority of applicants and are a pretty safe bet for B students.

Acceptance rates can tell you something about a university's selectivity, but it also helps to look at the academic profile of the admitted class to get a sense of where you stand. For example, in the following table, College A has a 35 percent acceptance rate and College B accepts 30 percent of applicants. However, College A might have a more competitive applicant pool and admit a class with stronger credentials. Ultimately, College A might be harder to get into as a B student, especially since the majority of accepted students graduated in the top 10 percent of their high school classes. Therefore, it is important to look at *both* acceptance rates and the credentials of the accepted students.

Sample Comparison of Acceptance Rates and Credentials of Accepted Students

	COLLEGE A	COLLEGE B
Acceptance Rate	35	30
Percentage of Admitted Students in Top 10 Percent of High School Class	52	38
Average 25th–75th Percentile Critical Reading SAT Scores	570–670	550–640
Average 25th–75th Percentile Math SAT Scores	610–680	560–630
Average 25th–75th Percentile Writing SAT Scores	600–690	610–670
Average 25th–75th Percentile ACT Scores	26–31	25–29

COMPONENTS OF A COLLEGE APPLICATION

Unfortunately, most students will find that there isn't just one simple "college application" that they can fill out and send to all the colleges on their lists. The closest thing we have is the Common Application, which is accepted by nearly five hundred colleges and can be found online on the Common Application website (www.commonapp.org). Some of these colleges also require supplements to the Common Application that may or may not include additional essays. In addition, many states like Maryland, California, and New York require their own applications and some private colleges may also require separate applications. While all these different types of applications may seem confusing, there is a great deal of overlap in terms of the questions that they ask applicants. A standard college application is comprised of several different parts:

- Student information (basic information about the student and parents, including where the parents went to college and what they do professionally)
- Essays
- Extracurricular activities
- Guidance counselor recommendation

- One or two teacher recommendations
- High school transcripts
- Standardized test scores
- Interview (Some colleges offer interviews, either on campus or with alumni.)
- Optional supplementary material like an art portfolio or music recording (These are usually sent to professors or teaching assistants to be evaluated, and then the evaluators send comments back to the admissions office.)

While each of these components is considered, academics (grades and test scores) are the most important part of the admissions process. However, all academic records are not created equal. Here are four things that can make someone a more desirable academic candidate:

1. **Rigorous courses.** Colleges want intellectually curious students who challenge themselves when given the chance. It may sound obvious, but admissions officers prefer high school students who take more advanced courses. In most cases, they look most closely at the five core high school subjects—science, math, English, history, and foreign language—and less at electives like music or art. Ideally, you should have four years of each of these subjects and push yourself to take at least some of the advanced courses that your school has to offer. (See chapter 7, Making Each Piece of Your Application Count, for more information on how admissions officers interpret the rigor of your transcript.) Your guidance counselor is the best source of information for what constitutes a rigorous college-prep course load in your school.

2. **An upward grade trend.** Admissions officers want to see improvement throughout the course of high school. If you had a rocky transition to high school but turned things around, you're likely to continue this positive trend into college. However, if your grades started off strong but dipped when the work got harder, admissions officers will wonder if you are cut out for

college-level work. You want to do whatever you can to have a strong finish.

3. **Outstanding guidance counselor and teacher recommendations.** Most college applications require a recommendation letter from your guidance counselor and one or two letters from high school teachers. These letters help admissions officers understand what kind of student you are. Do you contribute to class discussion? Do work well with other students? Do you do extra credit when it is offered? They can also be good places to explain any mitigating circumstances—illnesses, personal problems, and so on—that might have impacted your grades. Chapter 7 goes into more detail about these letters, but glowing recommendations can compensate for a few bad grades and add to the overall strength of your academic record.

4. **Great standardized test scores.** Admissions officers get applications from high schools all over the world. With so much variation among schools, they use standardized tests like the SAT and ACT to compare students. Needless to say, admissions officers prefer students with great test scores to those with poor scores. If your grades don't reflect your academic potential or ability, standardized tests can be another way to show colleges that you're smart.

STANDARDIZED TESTING TIMELINE AND TIPS

Individual colleges have different standardized testing requirements, so it can sometimes be difficult to make sense of all your options and plan ahead. Here are descriptions of the common types of tests as well as some strategies for test preparation.

SAT

The SAT is the most famous (or infamous) university admissions exam in the world. It consists of three separate sections, each of which is worth up to 800 points for a possible total of 2400. The critical reading section tests reading comprehension and vocabulary. The writing section measures grammar knowledge and requires a brief essay. The math section tests arithmetic, operations, algebra, geometry, probability, and statistics. A full-length SAT takes three hours and forty-five minutes to complete and is administered by the College Board seven times each year (January, March, May, June, October, November, and December).

Did you ever wonder how the SAT became a college admissions staple? For the first 250 years of their existence, Ivy League and selective colleges drew from certain "feeder" high schools where wealthy families sent their sons. When railroad travel became more accessible around 1900, these exclusive northeastern colleges wanted to find a way to attract smart and talented white men from different parts of the country. A Princeton psychologist named Carl Bingham adapted a multiple-choice exam used to sort army recruits for military assignment during World War I into a new product called the Student Assessment Test. This army test was an attractive blueprint for a college admissions exam because it tested general reasoning ability (instead of what you learned in high school) and could be mechanically scored because it was a multiple-choice exam. In the 1930s, administrators at Harvard instituted a National Scholarship Program to attract talented students from all parts of the country who could not otherwise afford to attend. Admissions officers found that the SAT coupled with high grades was effective in identifying gifted students across the country. The SAT has been dreaded by high school students ever since.

It's hard to know exactly how much money students spend on test prep, but estimates put the number at about $4 billion a year. The College Board has always contended that the SAT is a standardized exam that cannot be cracked or coached. However, a few years ago the organization began offering its own online prep course for $70. Why would the test writers who claim that their test can't be coached start offering their own prep course? This kind of confusing mixed message often frustrates students who are looking for straight answers about how to do their best on an exam that will help determine where they go to college.

Here's what we do know about the SAT:

- No one disputes that students can and should study for the SAT. The only question is about whether expensive test-prep options are worth their price compared to students' average score gains.
- Students who gain familiarity with the test can increase their scores. One of the benefits of attending prep classes or hiring a tutor is that you set aside time to focus on the SAT.
- The prep industry is unregulated and the data on average score gains is not checked by a third party. Always take these companies' claims with a grain of salt.

What's the best course of SAT preparation for most students? Do you need to pay for an expensive course or private tutor? Can you do just as well getting some books from the library and studying on your own?

The answers to these questions depend on what type of student you are. We know that it is important to study for this exam, so the question becomes this: are you capable of studying for the SAT on your own? Most courses offer twenty to thirty hours of instruction as well as several full-length practice tests. Can you make this kind of time commitment without the structure of a course? If the answer is yes, then you will probably be fine with a few prep books and a good SAT vocabulary list. If the answer is no, you need to find something more structured. The following table gives some information on three common test-prep options.

Common Test Preparation Options

CLASSROOM COURSE: $800 – $2,500	
PRO	**CON**
• Course curricula contain information that students need to be prepared for the SAT. • Students who attend complete a minimum number of study hours. • Many courses administer full-length practice exams in testlike conditions. • Students have access to an instructor who can answer questions.	• Courses don't always fit into students' busy schedules. • The quality of course instructors varies greatly, especially the largest, multinational tutoring companies that offer comparatively low faculty compensation. • Students do not receive individualized attention. • Courses are typically offered in more densely populated areas. (*Note:* Some companies are starting to offer courses via online videoconferencing programs like Skype so that might be an option for rural students.) • Classes may be overcrowded. • The quality of instruction materials may vary. • Many companies have been accused of administering inaccurate practice tests to manipulate students' score gains.

ONLINE COURSE: $30 – $1,000	
PRO	**CON**
• A wide range of prep options—from customized courses and video tutorials to basic skill-building exercises—is available. • Students can work around their schedules. • Many inexpensive options are offered. • Unlike classroom courses, many prep companies use their best instructors for online courses.	• Students must be self-motivated to take advantage of an online course. • Students can't always ask questions. • With so many options, it can be difficult to evaluate quality.

PRIVATE TUTORING: $100–$1,000 PER HOUR	
PRO	**CON**
• Individualized instruction is tailored to students' skill level and goals. • Good tutors not only teach, they motivate, troubleshoot, and manage time. • Tutors communicate with parents as well as students to help family members to support students' test-prep efforts.	• Costly. • Not always available in remote locations, although some tutors may agree to work with you online using a videoconferencing program like Skype. • Individual tutor quality varies. • Students can become overreliant on tutor and not take responsibility for their own learning. • Tutors don't always require students to take full-length practice exams, so they may not have the endurance to complete the test when the time comes.

The good news for low-income students is that there are several not-for-profit test-prep organizations that offer courses both in person and online. Many school districts offer prep courses to students, and non-profit organizations such as I Need a Pencil (www.ineedapencil.com) and Let's Get Ready! (www.letsgetready.org) offer free test prep to low-income students. You can check these test-prep class schedules and locations online.

ACT

Most selective colleges will consider the ACT in lieu of the SAT. The test is scaled from 1 to 36 and lasts two hours and fifty-five minutes with an optional thirty-minute writing section, making it a bit shorter than the SAT. There are four sections on the ACT: English, math, reading, and science. The English section overlaps with the writing section on the SAT and measures grammar and rhetorical skills like identifying sentences that are written in a similar style. The math is slightly more advanced than the SAT because it includes some trigonometry and focuses more on algebra and geometry. The reading section is similar to the critical reading section of the SAT and consists of four passages, one passage on each of the following topics: social studies, natural sciences, prose fiction, and humanities. The science section is the most different from the SAT; it assumes a general familiarity with topics in biology, chemistry, physics, and earth science, but it mostly tests your ability to interpret data, understand research summaries, and distinguish between conflicting viewpoints.

Because the questions are written in more straightforward language and tend to measure the practical over the abstract, the ACT is commonly perceived to be closer to what most students get in school, while the SAT is more like a puzzle or word game. These differences date back to the origins of the two exams. The SAT enjoyed a monopoly in the standardized testing world until 1957 when E. F. Lindquist, a professor at the University of Iowa, introduced the American College Testing Program (ACT). Unlike the SAT, which tested general math and verbal ability, the ACT was comprised of four sections for each of the primary high school subjects: math, English, social studies, and natural sciences. This type of assessment appealed to midwestern universities that traditionally emphasized high school course content in admissions decisions. The ACT allowed schools like the University of Michigan and the University of Wisconsin to evaluate and admit talented students from out of state, which served to increase their national prominence. Over the years, most selective colleges have opted to accept both the ACT and SAT exams.

The chart on the opposite page summarizes some of the basic differences between the SAT and ACT.

As a rule of thumb, students who enjoy fast-moving puzzles and word games might want to consider the SAT and students who study hard and are more comfortable with practical, content-based questions might do better on the ACT. But the truth is, there is a great deal of overlap between these exams and they are fairly equivalent, which is why most colleges will accept either exam.

Lately I've been seeing more students who are advised to take both exams with the logic being that the more tests you take, the more chances you have to get a high score. I disagree. Students are so overscheduled and overtested these days that I just don't see the value in voluntarily adding more exams to your plate when there is absolutely no benefit in terms of college admissions. It's better to focus your energy on studying for one and doing well instead of spreading yourself thin and not doing your best on either exam.

A Comparison of the SAT and the ACT

	SAT	ACT
Duration	3 hours and 45 minutes	2 hours and 55 minutes with optional 30-minute writing section
Number of sections	9 plus an essay	4 plus an optional essay
Fast-paced questions	No	Yes
Questions written in more straightforward language	No	Yes
Questions tend to be more abstract	Yes	No
Tests grammar	Yes	Yes
Tests vocabulary	Yes	No
Tests reading comprehension	Yes	Yes
Tests algebra	Yes	Yes
Tests geometry	Yes	Yes
Tests trigonometry	No	Yes
Tests writing skills	Yes	Optional
Tests ability to interpret scientific data	No	Yes
Tests ability to interpret scientific research	No	Yes
Penalizes students for guessing	Yes	No
Favors students with a longer attention span	No	Yes
Favors students who have difficulty processing information	No	Yes
Favors students with good vocabularies	Yes	No
Favors students with quick reading speed	No	Yes
Colleges superscore different sections	Yes	Sometimes

SAT Subject Tests (also referred to as SAT 2s) are hour-long, multiple-choice exams that are offered by the College Board and required at only the most selective colleges. There are twenty different exams that students can choose from, and most colleges that do require SAT 2s as part of their admissions process only require two to three exams. The following is a list of all the subject tests offered:

- Literature
- U.S. History
- World History
- Math Level 1
- Math Level 2
- Biology
- Chemistry
- Physics
- French
- French with listening

- Spanish
- Spanish with listening
- German
- German with listening
- Modern Hebrew
- Italian
- Latin
- Chinese with listening
- Japanese with listening
- Korean with listening

Students can take up to three exams on a single test date. Most of the exams are offered seven times a year on the same dates that the College Board offers the SAT 1 Reasoning Exam (aka the SAT). You can check the test dates on the College Board website.

Since only the most selective colleges require SAT Subject Tests for admission, if you plan to apply to colleges that accept more than 35 percent of students, it's a pretty safe bet that you won't need these tests. However, you still might want to take them for two reasons. First, a good score can demonstrate that you have mastered a particular subject in high school. Second, many colleges will award you credit or placement based on good SAT Subject Test results. If you are particularly strong in one of the subjects that the SAT 2 tests, you should go to the College Board website and take a free practice exam to see where you stand. Remember, you can and should study for these tests, so take your practice score as a baseline and work hard to bring it up.

ADVANCED PLACEMENT EXAMS

Advanced Placement, or AP, exams were first introduced in the 1950s as a way for talented high school seniors to gain college credits in one or two subjects in which they excelled. They have since grown tremendously in popularity with over one million students now taking these exams each year. Typically, a student who takes an AP exam has also completed a year-long AP course in the subject in preparation for the exam. However, the College Board allows anyone, including home-schooled students, to register for the exam. Unlike SATs, ACTs, and SAT 2s, the AP exams are only offered once each year in May (presumably after students have completed the course leading up to the exam). You can check the AP exam dates on the College Board website (http://apcentral.collegeboard.com/apc/Controller.jpf).

Students can choose from thirty-four different AP exams:

- Art History
- Biology
- Calculus AB
- Calculus BC
- Chemistry
- Chinese Language and Culture
- Computer Science A
- Macroeconomics
- Microeconomics
- English Language
- English Literature
- Environmental Science
- European History
- French Language and Culture
- German Language and Culture
- Comparative Government and Politics
- U.S. Government and Politics

- Human Geography
- Italian Language and Culture
- Japanese Language and Culture
- Latin: Vergil
- Music Theory
- Physics B
- Physics C: Electricity and Magnetism
- Physics C: Mechanics
- Psychology
- Spanish Language
- Spanish Literature
- Statistics
- Studio Art: 2-D Design
- Studio Art: 3-D Design
- Studio Art: Drawing
- U.S. History
- World History

With so many different subjects being tested, the format of the AP exam is not consistent across the board. AP art, for example, requires students to complete and submit an art portfolio, while history exams include multiple-choice and essay questions. The College Board website has more specific descriptions of the exams, but you should also talk to your AP teacher about the exam and course content, if you are considering signing up.

AP exams are graded on a scale of 1 to 5, and colleges have different policies when it comes to awarding students course credit based on their performance on the AP exam. The most generous schools will grant students college credit if they score a 3 or higher on the test. This is great because it gives students a cost-saving option for college credits. However, because of the growing number of students who take AP exams, some colleges have been more reluctant to give students credit for these exams because of the potential loss to their revenue stream. Still, even if you end up at a college that does not award credit for AP exams, most will at least use these exams for placement, so you won't have to repeat the course you took in high school and can move on to things that interest you.

SCORE CHOICE, SUPERSCORES, AND OTHER STANDARDIZED TESTING REPORTING STRATEGIES

What if you take an exam and don't do well? Do colleges see all your scores? Do they hold a low score against you if you retake the test and do better? Like many other things in the college admissions process, score-reporting policies can be confusing for students. Years ago the College Board required students to send all their scores when they applied to college. Then they switched to something called *score choice*, which allowed students to select which test scores they wanted to submit. Now, the College Board is letting the colleges decide whether or not they want students to submit all their scores. Every college is different, so you'll have to check each school's policy when you apply and proceed according to its stipulations.

If you're not happy with your SAT score, it usually helps to take it again if you think you might do better. (However, I wouldn't recommend taking it more than three times—your score isn't likely to improve significantly at that point and a good score is diminished when you take the test too many times.) In general, colleges will *superscore* your SATs, meaning that they will take the highest critical reading, writing, and math score regardless of when you received it. A student who gets a 600 on critical reading, a 550 on writing, and a 580 on math in May, and then gets a 630 on critical reading, a 570 on writing, and a 550 on math in June will have a superscore of 1780 on her SATs. Her superscore is the highest combination of all her scores. Some colleges—though not as many—will superscore the ACT exam as well. Check with the colleges to which you're applying to find out about their super-score policies for the ACT.

Colleges superscore these exams because they want to boast about their students' academic prowess. Most schools will report the average range of SAT scores in each category. It looks more impressive if they say "50 percent of our students scored a 600 or above on every section of the SAT" and omit the part about how these students may not have received these scores in a single exam.

For SAT Subject Tests, colleges decide if they require students to report all scores or if they allow students to select the scores they want to submit. (Some high schools include test scores on transcripts, so you might not get a choice even if the college technically allows you to choose.) The College Board website (www.collegeboard.org) has a comprehensive list of each school's reporting requirements. Unfortunately, every college is different, so you'll need to check each school on your list to see how it wants standardized testing scores sent. Since you may be considering taking an SAT Subject Test before you have the list of colleges to which you will apply, a good rule of thumb is to assume that you will have to report the result of the exam. If you think you'll do well, go for it. If you have major doubts, it might be best to wait or skip it since these exams are not required at most colleges.

For Advanced Placement exams, colleges allow students to self-report their scores in their applications, and they may recommend *but do not require* that students report all of their AP test results. If you are enrolled in an AP course but choose not to report your score, admissions officers will probably assume that you did not do well on the exam. If you took an AP test even though you were not enrolled in an AP course, then there won't be any indication that you took this exam unless you decide to report your score on your application. AP exams—especially in subjects for which you were not enrolled in an actual AP course—are not as high stakes as SAT Subject Tests. They can really only help you demonstrate your mastery of a subject, since you don't have to report the results.

LOOKING BEYOND ACADEMICS

While important, grades and test scores are not the only things that admissions officers look at when making their admissions decisions. Here are some other things that matter:

- **Extracurricular activities/leadership.** Admissions officers want passionate, active students who will have a positive impact on campus. They know the difference between someone who joins a bunch of different clubs just to pad their resume and a student who is deeply invested in activities that matter. Students who are leaders in their communities are going to be favored over those who are not.

- **Essays.** The college essay is your chance to let the admissions office get to know a little more about who you are and how you'll contribute. No one ever got into a college *just* because of a great essay, but a great essay can make the difference for a borderline candidate.

- **Showing interest in the school.** Everyone wants to be loved, and college admissions officers are no different. They want to choose students who are excited about their school and are more likely to attend. Students who visit campus, sign in at college fairs, go to in-school information sessions, and correspond with admissions officers are more likely to get their attention. If you are really excited about a school, be sure to let them know.

- **Applying early decision/early action.** One of the best ways to show a college that you really love it is to apply early. Research suggests that it is easier for a B student to get into a college if he applies early. Chapter 6 discusses how colleges use early admissions programs to build their classes and explains the various advantages and disadvantages of the different types of early admissions policies.

- **Having a "hook."** Admissions officers have many institutional priorities to consider, including building good athletic teams, having a diverse class, and promoting alumni satisfaction by admitting a high percentage of alumni children. Students who have these "hooks" are going to be at an advantage in the admissions process. If you're an athlete, a student of color, or a legacy applicant, see chapter 9, Getting the Red-Carpet Treatment, to understand more about how these things can help you in the admissions process.

- **Being a good match for the school or program.** If you are applying to an undergraduate business school, it helps to be strong in math and have some business experience; if you are looking at nursing programs, it helps to have good science grades and some hospital volunteer hours on your resume. Admissions officers at specialized programs are looking for students who will excel in a particular field. They may be willing to overlook some bad grades in courses that aren't relevant if you have a clear academic and/or extracurricular strength that makes you a good match for the school or program.

- **Interviews.** Some colleges offer on-campus interviews and others will give you the opportunity to interview with alumni in your hometown. The importance of the interview varies among colleges, but making a great impression on your interviewer can sometimes tip the scale in your favor.

CHAPTER 4 ACTION STEPS

❏ Look at both the acceptance rates and the academic profile of admitted students when evaluating your chances of getting into a particular college.

❏ Understand that all students are not created equal; rigorous courses, upward grade trends, teacher recommendations, and standardized tests can distinguish one student from another. Improve your overall academic profile by focusing on boosting your credentials in these areas.

❏ Ignore anyone who tells you that you can't prep for standardized tests. You should study for these tests and know your test-prep options.

❏ Because most colleges use superscores, it pays to take the SAT twice or even three times, if you think you can do better on one or more sections of the test.

❏ Understand what colleges look for beyond academics and use the tips in this book to help you make the most of the rest of your application.

CHAPTER 5

PAINLESS WAYS TO BEEF UP YOUR APPLICATION

When I was in my early twenties, my father, an avid hiker, generously offered to take my siblings and me on an amazing (and challenging) four-day hike along the Inca Trail. On the eve of our trip, I sat in a Peruvian hotel introducing myself to our fellow tour group participants. As I went around the room, I heard stories about their six-day running regimens, organic diets, and the high-tech gear they had purchased in advance of the trip. My "gear" consisted of old boots and workout clothes, and I couldn't remember the last time I had been to the gym. I felt like the only one who didn't get the memo that this was a serious endeavor that required some advance planning.

Fortunately, I didn't panic. I kept my head down, put one foot in front of the other, and made it to the summit with the group.

You may feel like I did on the eve of my hike, like you have no hope of catching up to all your classmates who have been thinking about and planning for college since they entered high school. Of course, in an ideal world, everyone would undergo a thoughtful and thorough planning process. But that's not the world we live in. If you feel like you're coming to the table late—say, at the end of your junior year or even as a senior—don't be intimidated. There is still time for you to get in the game and present yourself to college admissions committees in the best possible light.

LEARN HOW TO STAND OUT

Colleges want students who are change makers, students who can get things done. That's why virtually every college prefers applicants who exhibit leadership qualities. These include taking charge, motivating others, setting and meeting organizational goals, showing initiative, and being a force of good in your community.

Since students spend most of their time in school, this is a great place to start becoming a leader. You don't need to be class president or captain of the football team to demonstrate that you have what it takes to lead. Start by taking a survey of the things that you're already doing—the things that you *enjoy* doing—and see where there might be opportunities for you to take your involvement to the next level. Why not run for the presidency of the Spanish Club if you're going to all the meetings anyway or become an editor of the school paper if you're already writing articles? If you choose activities that interest you, it is easy to invest the extra time and energy to stand out in them.

It's not enough to have the title of "president" or "secretary" of a club, however. You have to *do* something with your newfound position to really be a leader. One student I worked with wanted to raise money for breast cancer research as his mother was a breast cancer survivor. He launched a campaign to compile his classmates' and teachers' personal stories of how they had been impacted by the disease into a self-published book whose proceeds went to benefit the cause. Another student had a very hard time identifying his "passion," but he knew he liked toys when he was a kid so he volunteered to run his school's annual Toys for Tots holiday drive. Instead of doing things the way they had always been done, he recruited local stores to donate merchandise in exchange for free ad space in the school newspaper and broke all previous donation records in the process. These students knew that leadership isn't about what you write on your resume or how many hours you spend on the basketball court; it's about the ability to invest in something you care about, to spot opportunities, and to make an impact when you put your mind to it.

Notice that both of these students also had a personal connection to the causes they chose, even if it was something as simple and pleasant as memories of opening toys on Christmas morning. What are the issues in your life that matter to you? Are you upset about the budget cuts at your public school? Do you want more local public spaces for students to exhibit their artwork, play music, or just hang out? Do you think it's important that all residents of your town have Internet access?

Pick an issue that you really care about, something that you want to see changed. Then get involved. Research organizations that work for causes that you support. Reach out to them on email or pick up the phone and call their offices. Spend some time learning about their work. (If you pick the right cause, this should be enjoyable.) Once you've established some personal relationships, look for opportunities to introduce new initiatives that build on the work that they are already doing.

Kelly is a great example of someone who embodies this approach. When we first met, she was a high school junior in treatment for an eating disorder. Because she lived in a community where eating disorders were very common, Kelly not only was concerned about her own recovery but also wanted to promote a healthy body image to other girls (including her younger sisters) who might be prone to anorexia or bulimia. Kelly decided to reach out to the National Association of Eating Disorders and learn more about their work. She then organized a series of events in her community to raise awareness about the issue; lobbied for the middle school to show *Someday Melissa,* a powerful documentary about anorexia, to all students in health class; and created an eating disorder peer counselor network at her high school. Kelly was happy to do these things because she genuinely cared about eating disorder prevention and awareness. She got into every college to which she applied because she was a unique, interesting applicant who had the potential to make a difference on college campuses, just as she had at her high school.

In his book *How to Be a High School Superstar*, Cal Newport makes a case that, when it comes to college admissions, it is more important to be an interesting applicant than it is to be a good student. Having read hundreds of applications to Dartmouth, I tend to agree with Newport. The most interesting applicants—the B students who get into Stanford, for example—are the ones who make admissions officers ask themselves, "How did she *do* that?" Newport gives some examples, like a sixteen-year-old who lobbied United Nations delegates for environmental reform and a high schooler whose technology-based health curriculum was implemented by ten states.

Lobbying at the UN? Developing a curriculum that was implemented in ten states? I know these examples probably sound a bit outrageous to many high school students, but you don't have to make headlines to learn something from Newport's approach. *You* can focus on things that are genuinely important to you and avoid taking on a laundry list of activities that you don't enjoy. For example, if you love photography, perhaps you could put on a "solo show" at your local church or community center and even solicit donations for a cause that you care about by selling your prints. Or, if you are passionate about the latest technology gadgets, start a Technology Club at school for fellow technology geeks or write a "tech" column for your high school newspaper. The point? You can focus on a few things without overextending yourself and build off the activities and interests that you already enjoy.

When it comes to extracurricular activities for college admissions officers, it's quality over quantity that matters. Admissions officers can spot students who are spread too thin or just going through the motions because their recommenders don't write about how they have made a difference in their communities. Another reality is that many of these overinvolved students tend to look alike on paper, which is a negative when you're trying to get an admissions officer's attention. If you focus on endeavors that you enjoy and care about, you are more likely to have a real, positive impact. Staying focused is one of the best things you can do to make yourself stand out—and to set yourself up to take advantage of opportunities when they present themselves.

In chapter 7, Making Each Piece of Your Application Count, I will talk more about how to craft the "narrative" of your college application. The *narrative* is the story you tell about how the different pieces of your life fit together and why they all make you someone who will excel at a particular college. Many students will want to include their academic interests and career goals as part of their narratives. Internships are a great way to enhance this part of your application. An admissions officer is more likely to believe that you have a passion for environmental law or graphic design if you have some experience in these fields.

When it comes to your college applications, the ideal type of internship is housed at an organization with a selective high school internship program because this shows admissions officers that you earned this position rather than happened to know someone who worked there. For example, the Manhattan district attorney's office invites junior and senior high school students who reside on the island to apply for a summer internship. Many congresspeople and local politicians also take on high school interns as will professors who might need some help in their lab or with some basic research. Your high school guidance counselor probably has information on these types of opportunities.

If you can't find a formal internship program, be prepared to be resourceful. As a high school student with no previous work experience and a limited window of availability, you'll most likely have to start with an unpaid internship. But even those can be tough to get; you'll be competing with college students who are in a similar boat. Make a list of all the people you know with interesting jobs. You might be surprised by how many possibilities there are in your personal network—your journalist aunt or stockbroker family friend, for example.

If you don't have many connections, you could also try to email people you find on the Internet that are doing interesting things. Reaching out to a busy stranger takes some finesse, however. First, tailor your email in a way that shows you have a familiarity with her work and how your personal interests and experiences will make you a valuable intern. Give her clear information about your availability and commitment level and don't demand a specific job like "I would love to work on your magazine's photo shoots," or "I am interested in helping you present legal cases at trial." Interns should be humble, flexible, and available for whatever projects the office needs.

Here is a sample letter that one of the students I worked with used to reach out to his congresswoman:

> To Whom It May Concern,
>
> I am writing to inquire about the possibility of pursuing a fall internship at the District Office of Congresswoman Irina Ros-Lehtinen. As a resident in Florida's 18th Congressional District, I have been deeply impressed with the Congresswoman's efforts on behalf of her constituents and would be honored to support her work as an intern.
>
> For as long as I can remember, I have been keenly interested in both national as well as international politics. I closely followed Congresswoman Ros-Lehtinen's role in the health care debate and am excited about her participation in the new Latino-Jewish caucus, as I am a member of both of these communities in South Florida. On the international stage, I have always been interested in the ongoing conflict in the Middle East and sincerely admire Congresswoman Ros-Lehtinen's involvement in attempts to establish a lasting peace in the region. I cannot imagine a better opportunity to gain an understanding of these and other meaningful issues than interning for Congresswoman Ros-Lehtinen.
>
> I am currently a junior at [a local] high school. I have spent more than a year doing policy analysis in a forensics/debate course where I had to explore the latest piece of legislature being debated in Congress and examine its possible effects on a particular topic area.
>
> I have also had previous work as an in-store employee at Papa John's Pizza during the summer of 2011. As an in-store employee, I learned the importance of good time management, especially on busy days when multitasking was essential. I also learned how to be an effective part of a team.
>
> I am available every Monday and Wednesday afternoon. I look forward to hearing from you at your earliest convenience.
>
> Sincerely,
> An Eager Intern

WHY HAVING A JOB IS A PLUS

Not everyone can afford to do an unpaid internship or participate in an expensive academic summer program. Lots of students work to contribute to their household finances—and even if you're just working for pocket money, having a job can still be a plus on your college application. Admissions officers know that having a job means having responsibilities. You are required to show up on time, work a certain number of hours, get along with coworkers, and perform assigned tasks. While this might not sound very worthwhile at first, these things are actually important signs of maturity. Adults know that success in life is just as much about showing up and being able to work with other people (even when the work isn't "fun") as it is about being smart or creative. Having a job shows that you understand these requirements.

Though it may not seem as glamorous as a museum internship or passionate political activism, a real job—things like pizza delivery, bookstore clerk, and waiting tables—can actually be more rare in the selective college applicant pool than some of the things we think of as being more interesting. Research suggests that the majority of students at selective colleges come from upper and upper-middle income households in which high school students don't need to work to help their families pay their bills. So having a job not only demonstrates maturity, it may also help you stand out.

THE BENEFITS OF ONLINE AND COMMUNITY COLLEGE COURSES

Are you a B student who gets As in English and history and Cs in math and science? If so, you might want to consider strengthening the weaknesses in your academic profile by supplementing your regular high school courses with online courses. There are several advantages to this approach. First, online and community college courses offer a wider range of options than your high school. Maybe you didn't do very well in chemistry, but you're really interested in other sciences like geology or oceanography. Maybe the Chaucer and Shakespeare English assignments weren't your thing, but you feel really excited about Beat poetry or the literature of hip-hop. At the end of the day, college admissions officers want to admit people who are smart and interesting. Taking the initiative to supplement your regular course work with online and community college courses that interest you shows them that you are intellectually curious and can succeed in an academic environment under the right circumstances.

If you can fit it into your schedule and the costs aren't prohibitive, take a supplementary course for credit so that you can include the grade in your application. Most community colleges offer courses during the summer and in the evening, which won't interfere with your regular high school schedule. Online courses are even more flexible, and prestigious colleges like Stanford, Brown, and UCLA all offer distance-learning options that come with a graded transcript. If your budget prohibits you from paying for an online or college course, you can still take advantage of this option. Universities like MIT, Carnegie Mellon, and the University of California at Berkeley offer free online courses to anyone who wants to take them. These courses aren't interactive and there's no graded work. However, if you make the commitment to watch all of MIT's Introduction to Engineering videos, be sure to put that on your college application and communicate this to your guidance counselor.

SUMMER PROGRAMS

The summer between junior and senior year is a crucial time for an ambitious college applicant. Though there are several advantageous ways to use this time, academic summer programs can be a good bet. Some of these programs have deadlines as early as January or February of junior year, but many of them allow you to apply right up until the program begins in July or August.

There are two types of academic summer programs that show colleges you're interested in doing something academic in your free time. The first are programs where you go to a college campus and take a range of liberal arts courses, like philosophy, psychology, or art history. The experience is similar to what you might have if you were a student at the university. You'll get a sense of what it's like to live in a dorm, take college-style (and in some cases college-level) courses, and hang out on a college campus. The second type of summer program is subject focused. You participate in the program to learn something specific, whether it's architecture or zoology, and you take one or several courses in this area. These programs can be a good way to enhance your academic profile because they can help you take one of your interests to the next level. They also might help you clarify what you want to study in college because you can take courses like economics and engineering, which aren't always offered in high schools.

A very popular type of subject-based summer program is the foreign language program. Many of these programs take place abroad. The best ones give you the opportunity to live with a host family and really immerse yourself in the language and culture of a particular country.

For-profit community service trips are also popular among high school students. Companies charge thousands of dollars for teens who want to go on a community service trip where they do things like build houses in Ecuador or help out in a Guatemalan orphanage. Though it's wonderful to get involved in service programs in developing countries, these programs won't gain you much credit in the college admissions office. In fact, many colleges view these programs in a negative light, as if you are trying to "buy" the community service credential when you're really just off having fun on a vacation with other teens. If you're really passionate about community service, try looking for nonprofit or religious organizations that do not require students to pay a fee to participate in service abroad. You can also find ways to make a difference in your school or community. Making a commitment to local endeavors shows the admissions committee that you don't need deep pockets to have an impact on the world around you.

How can you get more information about these academic summer programs? The best place to start is your high school guidance office, which might have some information about programs that other students in your school have enjoyed. If that doesn't work, the Internet can be a good resource. Summer program search engines like Enrichment Alley (http://enrichmentalley.com) or Peterson's Summer Programs (www .petersons.com/college-search/summer-programs-camps-search.aspx) can help you find opportunities that might fit your interests. You can also do some straightforward Internet sleuthing, provided you know which college you're interested in studying at or what topic you might want to study. For example, Google "Boston University Summer Programs for High School Students" and you'll be surprised to see that BU offers residential summer programs for ninth through twelfth graders in almost every subject you can imagine. Type "Theater Programs for High School Students" into a search engine and you'll have dozens of programs to choose from. Some high schools or community centers also host fairs for representatives from various summer programs to distribute their materials. If you are lucky to have access to one of these, take advantage of it and ask the reps all the questions you have about their programs.

After you've focused on a few programs that fit your interests and budget, make a spreadsheet that helps you keep track of program requirements and deadlines. Create columns for application requirements—things like essays, transcripts, standardized test scores, teacher recommendations, and financial aid forms—as well as deadlines for each of these programs. Then get out your calendar and set intermediate deadlines for yourself. For example, if you are applying to three programs with two essays each and the deadline is in six weeks, you need to write one essay each week. (Don't forget to leave time for editing, especially for the selective summer programs!) Also, make sure you stay organized about the other materials you need to send, such as official transcripts and standardized test scores. Writing things down on a calendar or spreadsheet will help you stay on top of deadlines.

Unfortunately, not all summer programs for high school students offer financial aid, so make sure that you can afford the program before you invest too much time in the application. If you find that you really can't afford to participate in any of these programs, don't worry. There are plenty of other painless ways to beef up your college credentials that you can do free of charge.

SELF-DIRECTED ACTIVITIES

Steve Jobs, Mark Zuckerberg, Oprah—many of the big visionaries over the past few decades were able to change the world precisely because they did their own thing and worked outside of the system. They have taught us that there are many different paths to success, and you don't have to be a joiner to be interesting or have something to offer. If you're more of an introvert, there are still many worthwhile, self-directed activities that you can pursue that will also impress the admissions committee.

A common solitary activity is writing, and I meet students all the time who simply love to write. They look forward to their English class assignments, secretly enjoy writing thank-you cards when they get presents, record their observations in a journal, submit articles to the school newspaper, and so on. Admissions officers know that writing is an essential part of a successful academic experience in college. If you're truly passionate about writing, there are several ways to take your passion to the next level. One of the easiest ways is to start a blog. The best blogs have a theme—say, "high school life" or "true stories from the babysitting front lines"—and give you a platform to discuss an issue or even just express yourself in an interesting and thoughtful way. The key to blogging is to be regular about it. You should aim for at least three posts a week. Post the entries you really like on Facebook, or email them to your friends and family so that you get some followers. Not only is blogging great practice for your potential future writing career, it is also a fantastic way to get feedback on your work because it is public. You can even try out some college essay ideas on your blog! Just be sure that you don't write anything that you wouldn't want an admissions committee to see because someone might actually look it up.

Music is another activity that students pursue "just for fun" that can look good on your college application. If you spend hours after school practicing guitar, writing songs, or playing in a band in your friend's garage, make sure to include these hours in the "activities" section on the Common Application. If you're confident about your abilities, go ahead and record a couple of songs and send the recording to admissions offices. You don't have to be a classical musician or an award-winning marching band tuba player to have something to offer. College towns are famous for having all kinds of live music, so don't be afraid to show admissions officers that this is an area where you can contribute.

Lately I've been meeting more and more students who are into self-directed computer programming—especially for iPhone applications. I worked with one student who had the frustrating experience of designing an app that provides nutritional information for food only to find that he was late to the market and these apps already exist. While this situation isn't ideal, it doesn't mean that this student's work was a waste of time. Not only did it give him practice in coding and designing, he could still put the hours he spent on this activity on his college application. If you're interested in creating an iPhone application but don't know exactly what type of app you want to make, a good idea is to approach the faculty of the technology department at your school and see if they need help with anything. Another student I know developed an app that students in his high school could download to help them keep track of the school's confusing schedule of final exams. This wasn't a mass-market product, but it did score him major points with school administrators and teachers, who were happy to praise him and his work in their recommendation letters.

Therein lies the key to self-directed activities—admissions officers will take notice if the adults who write your recommendation letters praise you for these pursuits. If you have a self-directed passion like poetry or photography, get out there and share it with the world. Be the singer-songwriter who performs at talent shows, write the iPhone app that everyone uses to figure out the best places to eat lunch off campus, or get permission to stage an independent art show in the old broom closet at school to show off your paintings. The more people who see your work, the more feedback you'll get and the more likely you will improve. This approach also allows the people writing your recommendations to appreciate your passion and help communicate how you can contribute to college life.

CHAPTER 5 ACTION STEPS

❑ Don't take on too many things at once. Staying focused is the best thing you can do to have an impact.

❑ If you are already a member of some clubs and organizations, identify the things you enjoy doing and volunteer for a leadership position.

❑ Embody the spirit of a leader by having a positive impact. Do things better than they have been done in the past.

❑ If you're not currently involved in clubs or activities, think about the issues that matter to you and reach out to organizations that have similar values. Learn about the work that is already being done to support this cause and look for opportunities to build off that work.

❑ If you invest your time in causes and organizations that you genuinely care about, your involvement won't feel like "work."

❑ Having a job shows that you can make a commitment and meet responsibilities; jobs can sometimes be distinctive on college applications because many high school students do not work.

❑ Find internships and summer programs that give you the opportunity to explore your interests outside of the classroom and build on the "narrative" of your application.

❑ Taking online and community college courses can help you improve your academic profile and allow you to show intellectual curiosity and initiative.

CHAPTER 6

MAKING THE MOST OF EARLY ADMISSIONS POLICIES

Approximately 70 percent of the top 281 colleges and universities that are ranked by *U.S. News and World Report* have some sort of early admissions policy. Under these policies, students may apply to their top-choice college early in their senior year, and they will receive a response from the college about six weeks later. The straightforward logic behind these policies is as follows: if you know that a school is your first choice, wouldn't it be nice to get the whole process over with as early as possible?

No matter what anyone tells you, your chances of being accepted at your first-choice college are almost always better if you apply for early admission. In fact, applying early is one of the best things that applicants can do to maximize their chances of admission. In 2004, Harvard professors Christopher Avery, Andrew Fairbanks, and Richard Zeckhauser looked at admissions data from the top 250 colleges and found that applying early is the statistical equivalent of a 100-point boost in SAT score. Data collected by the *New York Times* also reveals that admission rates from early decision schools are roughly twice as high as they are for regular decision. Many colleges publicly attribute this to the fact that the early decision applicant pool is stronger than the regular decision applicant pool. However, Avery, Fairbanks, and Zeckhauser actually found that the early decision applicant pool tends to have weaker grades and test scores. Therefore, applying early decision gives students a slight advantage in the admissions process on average.

It's not that colleges make huge exceptions for early applicants. It is important to understand that an unqualified applicant still won't get into an incredibly selective college just because she applied early. However, applying early can be a plus, especially for students who can compensate a bit for less-than-perfect grades by showing their love for a school. As I've stated multiple times, colleges are concerned about their selectivity. There are two things that contribute to selectivity: the number of applications that a college receives and the percentage of students who accept an offer of admission. The latter statistic is commonly referred to as a college's yield, and all colleges want to do their best to ensure a high yield. For example, although Boston University receives about ten thousand more applications than Harvard, they have to accept a much larger percentage of students because many more students will eventually turn them down. The yield on early decision students, however, is 100 percent as all of them have signed a form where they pledge to enroll if accepted.

Having worked in an admissions office, I believe that early admissions policies offer students another advantage as well. Early applicants do not risk falling victim to the fatigue that many admissions officers experience as the application reading season progresses. It's just human nature. At the beginning of the admissions cycle, their eyes are well rested, they are eager to learn more about the exciting new crop of applicants, and it's always nice to read the early application because admissions officers know that these students are serious about attending their college. However, as the cycle draws on, admissions officers can get burned out and the applications can start to look the same. As with many things in life, when it comes to college admissions, it's always better to be first in line. The following section breaks down the different types of early admissions programs as well as the pros and cons of each.

EARLY DECISION

Early decision is a binding agreement between the applicant and the college whereby the student applies to his first-choice college early (usually by November 1 or 15 of senior year) and receives a response approximately six weeks later. There are three different early decision admissions responses: acceptance, deferral, and rejection. An *early decision acceptance* means that you are required to enroll. An *early decision rejection* means that the college has turned you down. A *deferral* is like a lukewarm "maybe." The college releases you from the binding contract and agrees to look at your application again in the regular decision round. However, because you have the best chances of being admitted under the early decision program, it is important to note that the odds of getting in after being deferred aren't very good. I generally hear the same number from the admissions officers I talk to: around 10 percent of students deferred from early decision will eventually be admitted.

You should satisfy two important criteria before applying for admission under an early decision program:

1. You have selected your first-choice college and are absolutely certain that this is the school in which you want to enroll.
2. You have spent a great deal of time on campus, spoken to current students, sat in on a class, and are knowledgeable about the college's academic and extracurricular offerings.

It is crucial that students conduct this type of research before applying early decision because they could end up having to enroll. However, if you are certain about your selection, early decision is a great option because your chances of being accepted to your first-choice school are better, and you can get the whole process over with before you're halfway through senior year.

There is a lot of debate over whether early decision programs are appropriate for applicants who seek financial aid. The process of getting financial aid for college is sort of like shopping for a car—you know that you won't pay the sticker price, but until you visit dealerships, fill out the paperwork, and apply for loans, you can't exactly predict how much the car will cost. This kind of comparison shopping works for financial aid as well. Most "experts" argue that early decision programs hurt students who need financial aid because applying to a single school early decision does not allow them to compare financial aid offers.

This argument overlooks two important factors. First, if you happen to get into your early decision school but do not receive adequate financial aid, you might be able to negotiate for a better offer or even withdraw if you really can't make it work financially. Financial aid budgets are most flush at the beginning of the admissions cycle, so students who apply early decision might actually find that they receive a more generous need-based aid award. Second, as you'll see in chapter 11, most colleges are *need aware*, which means that if they are considering two equally qualified applicants, they will choose the one whose family can afford the full cost of attendance over the applicant who needs financial aid. Therefore, students who are not at the top of their class and plan to apply for financial aid might need the "boost" of early decision even more than their peers because it is already more difficult for them to get into need-aware colleges. If you fit into this category, you should ask yourself this question: Is it more important for me to have the best possible chance of getting into my first-choice school, or would I rather weigh financial aid offers at multiple colleges?

If you need financial aid to meet college costs, the best thing to do is to avoid any financial surprises by getting a financial aid estimate from any college to which you are considering applying early decision. That way you and your family will have better information on which to base your decision.

EARLY DECISION II

Some colleges have begun to offer a second round of early decision called "early decision II" (ED II). *Early decision II* follows the same rules as early decision except that the deadline is later, usually January 1 or 15. Of the 450-plus colleges that accept the Common Application, 15 percent have early decision II programs, and among these, there are some good options, such as Skidmore and Union, for B or B+ students. Early decision II offers the same admissions advantage for applicants because they are indicating that this is their first-choice college and that they will enroll if accepted. If any or all of the following apply to you, these programs may be especially beneficial for you:

- You have weak grades and need to boost your GPA in the first semester of senior year.
- You need to take (or retake) required standardized tests.
- You need more time to contemplate your college options.
- You need more time to consider your financial circumstances and your college budget.

Some students also use early decision II for what I like to call their "second first choice." This means that they apply early decision in November to their first-choice college, even though it is a big reach and they realize it is unlikely that they will be accepted. If they don't get in to that school early decision, they then apply to their second choice under the early decision II plan (assuming that this college is one of the schools that offers ED II) and receive the admissions benefit of early decision at their second first choice. Remember, early decision is binding whether it is the first or second round, so just be sure that you really love the college and can afford to attend if you choose to apply early decision II.

PROS	CONS
• Greater chance of being accepted to your first-choice college (assuming that you are a qualified candidate). • Know where you're going to college by December of your senior year (only for ED I).	• Must enroll if accepted—be sure this is your first-choice college! • Can't compare financial aid offers. • Colleges don't get a chance to consider first-semester grades for senior year or standardized tests taken after the fall (only for ED I).

EARLY ACTION

Early action programs are similar to early decision with one important difference: students are not required to enroll if accepted. Colleges that offer early action allow students to apply by an earlier deadline (usually sometime in November or early December of their senior year) and to receive a response between six and twelve weeks later. Similar to early decision programs, students who apply early action may be accepted, deferred, or rejected. If you are accepted under early action, you may still apply to other colleges and you have until May of senior year to consider your options and choose somewhere to enroll. If you get rejected under early action, you will no longer be considered for admission to that school. If you get deferred, the admissions committee will look at your application again in the regular decision round (along with an updated first-semester transcript from senior year as well as any new standardized tests).

Applying early action can be a good way to show interest in a school, and early action applicants tend to get accepted at higher rates than those who apply regular decision because these students are demonstrating interest in the school by getting their applications in early. However, because early action is not binding, the "bump" in the admissions process is usually less significant than if a student applies early decision. This means that early action schools are more likely to defer students if they want to see a complete first-semester transcript for senior year, and are more likely to accept early action students who have been deferred to the regular decision pool. So don't be too distraught if you don't get into your first-choice school early action; you are still in the running, especially if you follow the tips for deferred students that are included at the end of this chapter.

SINGLE CHOICE AND RESTRICTED EARLY ACTION

Because early action programs are not binding for students, some colleges have begun to place restrictions on how students use their early application options. Extremely selective colleges, like Harvard, Yale, Princeton, and Stanford, now have something called *single choice early action*, which means that applicants may not apply to any other *private* institution early, even though accepted students are not required to enroll. (*Note:* Single choice early action schools do allow students to apply early action to public universities to accommodate financial aid considerations.) Other schools, like Boston College and Georgetown, have initiated something called *restrictive early action*, which means that students may apply to any other colleges under early action but not early decision. Yes, these restrictions are confusing. The good news is that most early action colleges don't have these restrictions.

Pros and Cons of Early Action

PROS	CONS
• A good way to show that a particular college is high on your list. • May apply to several schools early. • Can compare financial aid offers. • Slightly higher chance of being accepted to your first-choice college (assuming that you are a qualified candidate). • May receive college acceptances early in your senior year.	• Colleges don't get a chance to consider first-semester grades for senior year or standardized tests taken after the fall. • Admissions advantage is not as great as for early decision.

YOUR EARLY ADMISSIONS STRATEGY

Now that you understand the advantage of applying early, it's important to consider this advantage when devising an application strategy that works for you. As I said, unqualified applicants can still be rejected early decision, so please do not look at these programs as lottery tickets to schools that are way out of reach. Instead, when you consider the selectivity of the colleges on your list, you can adjust those numbers in your favor if you apply early. For example, the early decision acceptance rate at Dickinson College was 53 percent and the regular decision acceptance rate was 28 percent in 2012 (the overall acceptance rate was 42 percent). The same goes for a highly selective college like Duke, which took 25 percent early and 11 percent of applicants in regular decision with an overall acceptance rate of 13 percent. *The Choice* blog of the *New York Times* (http://thechoice.blogs.nytimes.com) publishes great data from a few dozen selective colleges for both early and regular admissions programs. If data from the particular colleges on your list are not included in the compilation of the *New York Times*, call the admissions offices at the colleges on your list and ask for last year's acceptance rates for the early and regular applicant pools. Armed with this information, you will know whether applying early offers any real advantage.

Another negative of early admissions policies in general is that they force students to move the college search process up. It makes sense that you'll continue to mature and get to know yourself better as time goes on. Your "first choice" from junior year may not be the same school you'd choose as a senior. I once worked with a student who was completely gung ho on going to a big southern school—until she visited the Universities of Georgia, North Carolina, and Virginia and realized that she, coming from Evanston, Illinois, didn't feel at home in the South. If you don't feel ready to commit to a particular college, you'll need to carefully consider your early application strategy. You can still gain some of the benefits of applying early without necessarily making an ironclad commitment.

ROLLING ADMISSIONS

Rolling admissions means that admissions officers evaluate applications in the order in which they are received, and students receive admissions decisions on an ongoing basis throughout the year. Many large public universities and some less selective private colleges offer rolling admissions policies. If you're thinking of applying to a college with rolling admissions, it is in your best interest to get your application in early because you have a greater chance of being offered a spot when the class is less full at the beginning of the year. Rolling admissions can also be an advantage for students who are getting a very late start on their college applications as many of the less selective colleges with rolling admissions policies still have space available and will accept applications in the spring. If you find yourself in the position of wanting to send out applications in the spring of your senior year, you can do a search on either the Common Application (www.commonapp.org) or College Board (www.collegeboard.org) websites by application deadline and find a list of colleges that will accept late applications.

Students who apply to a rolling admissions program may be accepted, rejected, or waitlisted. Being placed on a college's *waitlist* means that you are a desirable candidate and qualified to attend, but there just wasn't enough room for you in the class. There is a great deal of variety in how colleges use their waitlists. Some accept hundreds of students and others take just a handful. The advice in this chapter on what to do if you've been deferred also works well for waitlisted students.

WHAT TO DO IF YOU'VE BEEN DEFERRED FROM EARLY DECISION OR EARLY ACTION

There are many reasons that colleges defer students who apply early to their regular decision applicant pool. The most common reason is that the student was qualified but did not stand out—perhaps there was a particular soft spot in the application (weak GPA, poor test scores, not enough leadership) or maybe the application was good overall but not distinctive enough to win a unanimous vote in an admissions committee. Many times admissions officers defer B students because they want to see how they do in the first semester of their senior year or see a new SAT score from a future test date. If you've been deferred, the good news is that you were qualified enough to make it to the next round. The bad news is that you still have not been accepted, which means that you need to do all that you can to convince the admissions office that you have something unique to contribute.

Early decision and early action deferrals mean slightly different things for applicants' chances of admission. Because the statistical advantage is greater for early decision applicants than for early action applicants, early decision applicants who get deferred have a lower chance of getting in during regular decision than early action applicants. Some colleges with early action actually make the first round harder than the second round because they don't have the same incentive to accept students early since these students are not required to enroll. As colleges see it, there's very little downside to evaluating qualified students with more information from senior year courses and tests.

PLACE A CALL TO THE ADMISSIONS OFFICE

Whether you've been deferred from early decision or early action, the first thing you should do is to call the admissions office and ask to speak to the regional admissions officer who read your file. I know that this suggestion may terrify many students, but try to get over your anxiety and realize that the best thing you can do for yourself at this point is to make the admissions officer see you as a unique person instead of a bunch of pieces of paper that make up an application. Try to resist the temptation to let your parents call for you. Colleges are looking to admit capable adults, so it is best for you to make the call—even if you are intimidated.

Once you get over your jitters and place the call, you'll likely speak with a receptionist who will take your contact information and have the admissions officer in charge of your region call you back. (If you have limited hours of availability, be sure to politely mention your best times to talk.) When you finally connect with the admissions officer, do your best not to sound too disappointed or entitled. Remember, you are still in the running, so stay positive. You should have two goals for this conversation: (1) to find out more about how you can improve your chances of admission in regular decision; and (2) to make a good impression on and a connection with the admissions officer who will likely be reading your application again.

Here are some do's and don'ts for you to consider when placing this call.

Do's and Don'ts for Calling Your Admissions Officer

DO	DON'T
Ask how you can improve your chances of admission.	Whine about how devastated you are because you didn't get in.
Use a polite, humble conversational voice.	Yell at or be short with the admissions officer.
Advocate for yourself by stating one or two specific things that you have to offer the college.	Complain about how much time you put into visiting the campus or working on your application.
Ask what percentage of deferred students is eventually admitted.	Demand to know what your chances of getting in are.
Stay positive about yourself.	Make excuses for that bad grade in math or your low critical reading score on the SATs.
Ask if the admissions officer wouldn't mind if you emailed her with updates.	Ask if you can meet with the admissions officer in person.
Restate that the college is your first choice and that you would love to attend.	Say anything negative about the school.

WRITE AN "UPDATE" LETTER

Most admissions officers will advise you to send an updated first-semester transcript and to write a letter to the admissions office with any updates on your academics or extracurricular activities. Have you kept up your grades? Are you taking a particularly challenging curriculum? Did you become president of a club or get a new part-time job? In the letter, you can also restate that this still is your first-choice college and outline some ways in which you feel you can make a contribution to the school. Don't make it all about what they can do for you or say that you want to go there because it's "such a great school" or because "the campus is so beautiful." Really put some thought into what makes this college unique and how you can make a difference on campus.

Here's an excerpt from a letter that Kate, a wonderful B student from New Jersey, wrote after getting deferred from Loyola College in Maryland:

> Since I applied to Loyola, I have continued the upward grade trend that I established in high school. My love of writing and literature has only grown stronger. However, I also found myself enjoying subjects like math and physics, two courses that had never really interested me in the past. In fact, I am proud to report that I just received a 96 on my most recent math test and a 97 on the last physics test I took. Rather than suffering from senioritis, I feel as if I really hit my stride this past year. If accepted, I know that I can make a contribution to my courses at Loyola.
>
> I have been keeping up with extracurricular activities as well. I remain an avid reader and have finished several new books in the past few months, including two books that I really loved, The Marriage Plot by Jeffrey Eugenides and Everything Is Illuminated by Jonathan Safran Foer. I am also continuing my community service and have especially enjoyed my involvement with the Bridge Program where I mentor underserved students. One of the things that I find so appealing about Loyola is the university's commitment to giving back. If accepted to Loyola, I will eagerly take advantage of similar community service programs that are offered on campus.

Kate does a great job of giving specific details (her most recent test scores, the books she recently enjoyed), and she focuses on how these things will help her contribute to Loyola. As a B student, she knows that she needs to make herself stand out by personalizing the letter. She focuses on the real things in her life—enjoying math and physics more than she thought she would—and doesn't sound like she's trying too hard to be someone she's not. As a result, she comes across as genuine and likable. By writing about her classes and other academic pursuits, Kate also seems smart. Her academic record may not be perfect, but it's obvious that she has intellectual potential.

SEND AN EXTRA RECOMMENDATION

It is not necessary to send additional letters of recommendation when you first submit your application, but asking a teacher from one of your senior-year courses to write one on your behalf after you get deferred can be a good way to show colleges that you are still interested in attending and that you are keeping up (or improving) your senior-year grades. Be sure to have your teacher focus on your current academic performance (do not succumb to senioritis) and to reiterate your strong desire to attend this college. Don't be shy about sitting down with your teacher to talk about specific highlights from the year or putting these thoughts down on paper. See chapter 7, Making Each Piece of Your Application Count, for tips on how to get great teacher recommendations.

GET SUPPORT FROM PEOPLE
OTHER THAN TEACHERS

If your recent academic performance hasn't been great or you don't have a teacher you can ask, a coach, adviser, or boss could also write you a letter as long as it adds something to the rest of your application. This works well for students who have taken on leadership roles during senior year—perhaps you're captain of the varsity basketball team or you broke the school record for breast cancer research fund-raising, for example—and want to show the admissions office that they continue to mature and have a positive impact on their communities. If you have a part-time job, your boss can also write a recommendation, especially if you've taken on more responsibility or made a contribution to the work-place that might translate to a college campus. Remember, this isn't just about what the college can do for you; it's also about how you can make a difference at that college.

Do you know anyone who graduated from your first-choice college? If so, now is the time to give them a call. Colleges care about their alumni because these are the people who give them donations and build their endowments. Therefore, most colleges find ways to involve alumni in the admissions process, most commonly by allowing them to offer alumni interviews. Alumni are also encouraged to write letters of recommendation on behalf of applicants whom they want to support. Unless you're getting a rave review from a member of the college's board of trustees or someone whose last name is featured on a campus building, it's best to save these letters in the event that you get deferred from early action or early decision. Having an alumnus or alumna write about you at this point shows that you're the type of person who might fit in well at the school because a graduate can vouch for you. It also shows that you're serious about attending because you went out of your way to ask for an alumni recommendation. Be sure to share your resume and transcript with the recommender and to highlight anything that you think should be mentioned. For example, you might want to point out an upward grade trend or particular leadership experiences that showcase your passion.

CHAPTER 6 ACTION STEPS

❏ Begin the college search process early so that you can hone in on your first-choice school and take advantage of the benefits of applying early decision.

❏ Pick an early decision school in the "sweet spot"—it shouldn't be so far out of your league that you have no chance, but it should be enough of a reach that the "bump" you'll get from committing early decision will yield an acceptance.

❏ Students who need financial aid should avoid any surprises by getting a financial aid estimate from any college to which they are considering applying early decision.

❏ If you are interested in a college that has the early decision II option, consider using this option for your "second first choice."

❏ It's usually good to add some early action schools to your list as well, if they allow you to apply to other colleges early.

❏ When looking at admissions data, get the acceptance rates for both the early and regular admissions programs so that you can assess the significance of the early admissions boost.

❏ If you apply to a college that reviews applications on a rolling basis, make sure to get your application in early!

❏ Take these actions if you get deferred from early decision or early action or if you are waitlisted:
  • Place a call to the admissions office.
  • Write an update letter.
  • Send an additional letter of recommendation.
  • Get support from alumni.

CHAPTER 7

MAKING EACH PIECE OF YOUR APPLICATION COUNT

Here's an all-too-common scenario: Mark and his parents visited several college campuses in the spring and summer of his junior year in high school. On each of these visits, they sat in on information sessions given by admissions officers who emphasized that colleges look at the student's "whole package" when making their admissions decisions—things like leadership, school spirit, and community contribution. These admissions officers seemed friendly and inviting, like the type of people who genuinely care about having interesting students on their campus. Mark went home from these visits feeling excited about applying to college. He was optimistic that he would be accepted at his reach school if he could just communicate all that he has to offer.

Now it's October of Mark's senior year. Mark knows that he wants to apply to his reach school early decision because it is his absolute first choice, and he wants the admissions committee to know how much he loves the school. With a couple of weeks to go before the early decision deadline, Mark decides to start working on his application. He spends about an hour filling out the Common Application, writes a few essays, shows them to his parents, ignores whatever feedback they give him *because* they are his parents, and presses the "submit" button a few days before the application is due.

Mark is shocked when he gets turned down from his reach school six weeks later. But anyone with any knowledge of what it takes to get into a reach school knows that Mark's approach just isn't going to cut it.

Many students think that the biggest investment of the college application process is visiting campuses and narrowing down the schools to which they will apply. But the truth is, it takes work to put together an application that showcases what you have to offer. Unfortunately, because this is your first time presenting yourself on paper and you don't have any benchmarks to compare it to, it can be difficult to even know what kind of standard you should have for your application or how much work you should put into it. Mark is a great example of a well-meaning applicant who was unable to meet the standards of his reach school because, at some level, he didn't even know what those standards were.

The first step to creating a great application is to get organized. I've seen many teenagers turn their parents' dining rooms into a college admissions "war room" with study guides and brochures growing out of every corner like weeds. But overloading on information can actually have a negative effect. By the fall of your senior year, you should have a working list of colleges so you don't need all that propaganda. If you follow the rule of only saving printed material that contains information that is not available on the Internet, you'll find that you can probably fit what you need into a single folder.

Once the clutter is gone, you can focus on what matters. Start by creating a chart to help you keep track of deadlines and application components. Here are some things that you should include.

Application Components and Deadlines

	COLLEGE A	COLLEGE B	COLLEGE C
Application Deadline			
Essay Requirements			
Teacher Recommendation Requirements			
Standardized Testing Requirements			
Standardized Testing Deadlines			
Supplemental Material Guidelines*			
Interview Information**			
Regional Admissions Officer Contact Info			
Additional Contacts at the College***			

*For students who wish to submit art portfolios, film projects, or musical recordings (more about this later in the chapter)
**On-campus, off-campus, name of interviewer, thank-you card sent, and so on
***Any active alumni, professors, students, or college administrators that you know

PRESENTING YOUR EXTRACURRICULAR ACTIVITIES: THE ACCOMPLISHMENTS DOC

The activities section on the Common Application has exactly ten lines and asks the applicants to fill in each line with the name of a sport, club, job, or volunteer organization. Next to that, you indicate how long you've been involved with the activity, how many hours per week and weeks per year you spend doing it, if you've held any leadership positions in this organization, and if you plan to continue this activity in college. There is also a short line—not even a whole sentence—for you to describe the activity. This is plenty of room for some activities like varsity soccer or Key Club because everyone knows what these are as they are found in almost every American high school. However, if you've won a dozen debate awards and competed in twenty different tournaments, just writing the word "Debate" won't accurately capture the nature of your involvement or achievement. In this case, a student should create and upload an "accomplishments doc" to fully explain her debating prowess. An *accomplishments doc* is basically a list of your high school activities with some meaningful descriptions (*Note:* Nothing before ninth grade counts on your college application.) Accomplishments docs can be great tools for students who want to show admissions officers the things they have to offer that are not captured on their transcripts.

Of course, the accomplished debater described above is truly exceptional, but how do most students know if they should include an accomplishments doc? Here are some simple guiding principles:

- If you have trouble filling in all ten lines on the activities section of the Common Application, then you do not need to complete an accomplishments doc. In fact, in doing so, you're likely to call *more* attention to the fact that you haven't done much outside of school.
- If you have exactly ten or eleven activities, you should create an accomplishments doc only if you feel that elaborating on some of these activities will enhance your application. Don't try to

inflate your activities in a way that isn't genuine or to make yourself sound like you're doing more than you do. Also, don't be redundant. If your accomplishments doc looks just like the activities section in the Common Application, don't send it.

- If the Common Application does not give you enough space to include all your activities, you should spend some time creating a document that provides additional information about your accomplishments. Keep the description as brief as possible and only include things that are significant. (If you went to a few meetings of Model UN in your freshman year, you can leave that out.)

As with everything on your college applications, you're going to want to devote some time to making your accomplishments doc as good as it can be. Students are often surprised by the number of drafts it takes to get this right. Because you are sending additional information that is not requested by the colleges, you have to craft a document that an admissions officer can skim and get a sense of how you're spending your time. The main challenge is to include as much information as possible in a concise, efficient, and clear way. I prefer a chart format with the following columns: Name of Activity, Description, Position Held, Grades, Hours/Week and/or Weeks/Year. Note that one of the columns says "Grades" instead of "Dates." Given that our goal is to make this easy to read or skim, it's better to write your grade number than the year. Don't ask admissions officers to do the math to figure out what year you were in ninth or tenth grade.

Another helpful thing to do is to break up your accomplishments doc into different categories that describe your extracurricular involvement—music, art, athletics, and so on—so that a reader can glance at the document and have a sense of the main types of things you do before he reads the particulars. In general, you want to list your activities in reverse chronological order so that the most recent activities appear first. There are some exceptions, however. For example, if you're a very athletic student who plays field hockey in the fall, basketball in the winter, and lacrosse in the spring, you'll want to group all your activities by sport instead of listing them in reverse chronological order. Here's an example of an accomplishments doc for a student who has pursued numerous activities in both sports and music; he grouped them by category to make it easier for admissions officers to read.

Athletics

ACTIVITY	DESCRIPTION	TITLE OR POSITION HELD	HOURS/WEEK	GRADES
Varsity Basketball	Selected to play forward for varsity high school team	Captain (11, 12) Forward (10, 11, 12)	15	10–12 Winter season
JV Basketball	Selected to play forward for junior varsity high school team	Captain (9)	12	9 Winter season
Varsity Field Hockey	Selected to play defense for varsity high school team; made county playoffs (11)	Defense (11, 12)	15	11, 12 Fall season
JV Field Hockey	Selected to play defense for junior varsity high school team	Defense (9, 10)	12	9, 10 Fall season

Music

ACTIVITY	DESCRIPTION	TITLE OR POSITION HELD	HOURS/WEEK	GRADES
New York State School Music Association	Selected to play baritone sax in the All-State Jazz Ensemble; jazz solo ratings of A+	Baritone saxophone	10	11, 12

ACTIVITY	DESCRIPTION	TITLE OR POSITION HELD	HOURS/WEEK	GRADES
Libral Youth Orchestra	Baritone sax for concert winds (9, 10) Baritone sax for jazz band (9)	Baritone saxophone	3–5	9, 10 School year
High School Band Officer	Maintain and strive to improve the quality of the band program, e.g., selecting music, adjusting schedules, and ensuring high morale	Vice president (11, 12)	Minimum of 1–2, depending on upcoming events	9–12

Notice how this student sometimes puts a range of numbers in the Hours/Week column. Colleges want to know how you spend your time, so this is an important piece of information to include in your accomplishments doc. However, not every activity meets for exactly the same amount of time each week. Feel free to put a range or your best estimation.

Informal or self-directed activities like reading, photography, or writing that you do in your free time should also be included in your accomplishments doc. Give brief descriptions like "Avid reader of historical literature; favorite books include *The Paris Wife* and *Devil in the White City*." These few sentences make me believe that you really do enjoy historical literature because you chose popular books instead of books that are commonly assigned for school. Therefore, you probably read in your free time. I once had a student who wrote "read fifty-two books in a single summer to win a bet; prize was more books." The specificity of the description not only convinced me that this student loves to read, it also conveyed that she has a sense of humor.

As we discussed in chapter 5, college admissions officers are generally looking for *interesting* students, so don't be shy about including any offbeat activities that you enjoy. Here's a great sample of a quirky "Hobbies and Interests" section from a student's accomplishments doc.

ACTIVITY/ INTEREST	GRADES	HOURS PER WEEK/ WEEKS PER YEAR	DESCRIPTION
Independent Science Research	10–12	7/52	Favorite magazines: *Scientific American, National Geographic* Topics of interest: roller coasters, solar energy, environment, material analysis, advanced microscopy
Roller Coasters	9–12	Varies	Have ridden on each of the 10 biggest roller coasters in the country; made and screened a short film about the physics of roller coasters at school talent show to raise money for breast cancer research
Adventurous Eating	9–12	N/A	Enjoy eating many strange foods such as chicken heart, roasted silkworm bugs, century-old preserved eggs, ostrich, alligator, etc.
Baking	9–12	2/52	Bake for birthdays, bake sales, family events; use principles of engineering to make elaborate cakes shaped like roller coasters and skyscrapers

Since this student is applying to engineering schools, it's interesting to see how she incorporates her academic pursuits into her daily life. The section on roller coasters is unique and memorable—you don't meet a genuine roller-coaster enthusiast every day—and it's wonderful that she branched out and made a short film about the physics of roller coasters and even baked roller-coaster cakes for fund-raisers. Adventurous eating is also something that stands out. Not many seventeen-year-old girls have the stomach for chicken hearts and century-old preserved eggs. She comes across as an interesting person, and that's the whole point of attaching an accomplishments doc.

YOUR TRANSCRIPT AND
HIGH SCHOOL PROFILE

Most students know that their academic record is a big part of their college application. However, few applicants understand how their academic performance is communicated to colleges. In addition to your high school transcript and standardized test scores, admissions officers also look at a document called the *high school profile* to assess how you have performed in the classroom as compared with your peers. High schools send school profiles along with student transcripts to help admissions officers interpret the meaning behind those letters or numbers.

Every school profile is different, but the College Board recommends that schools include the following pieces of information:

- School contact information
- District information (size, location, average family income, and so on)
- School information (size, grades taught, teachers' credentials)
- Information about the curriculum
- Description of the grading policy
- Standardized test results
- Percentage of graduates who immediately enter two-year and four-year colleges
- List of colleges that graduates have attended or been accepted to

Many students—especially in schools that do not have official ranking policies—will be surprised to see that their high school includes a grade distribution chart on its profile. It looks something like this:

There were 480 graduates in the Class of 2011.
- 46 earned a 4.0+.
- 150 earned 3.5–3.99.
- 76 earned 3.0–3.49.
- 112 earned 2.50–2.99.

- 55 earned 2.0–2.49.
- 41 earned less than a 2.0.

Students may also be surprised to learn that many high schools share their students' average SAT and AP scores with colleges. Here's a sample:

Standardized Test Results

76% OF THE CLASS OF 2011 TOOK THE SAT	54% OF THE CLASS OF 2011 TOOK THE ACT
Middle 50% Critical Reading: 490–610	Middle 50% Composite: 21–26
Middle 50% Math: 530–660	
Middle 50% Writing: 530–570	

Understanding how your academic record compares to that of your classmates will help you make a better assessment of your chances of being accepted to certain colleges (Naviance is also a great tool for this; see page 28, chapter 2). To learn more about your particular high school profile, here are some questions to ask your guidance counselor:

- Even though our school doesn't rank, do you report the grade distribution for the class? If so, where do I fall?
- Does the grade distribution take course rigor into account (this is also known as having "weighted" grades)?
- Do you report average standardized test scores to colleges? If so, where do my scores fall in the distribution?
- How many AP and honors classes does our school offer? How does my course load compare with other students at our school?
- What percentage of our graduates go on to college? Does our high school include a list of the specific colleges in the high school profile? (*Note:* Many admissions officers consider high schools where most graduates go on to selective colleges as more rigorous because they have a track record of preparing students for four-year colleges. If you are at a rigorous college-prep high school, they will interpret your grades accordingly.)

GUIDANCE COUNSELOR RECOMMENDATIONS

The recommendations that accompany your application are incredibly important and informative. A B student with truly outstanding recommendations may be preferable to an A student whose teachers can't be bothered to come up with more original adjectives than "hardworking" and "diligent." Even though you can't actually write your own recommendations, you can advocate for yourself and provide your recommenders with relevant information that will enable them to write better letters on your behalf.

Almost every college requires a guidance counselor recommendation. The form that accompanies the letter on the Common Application is fairly simple. The first page asks your guidance counselor for some basic contact information and includes a few lines where he will list your senior-year courses. The second page asks guidance counselors to provide important details about your academic record—your GPA, class rank, and course rigor. Your guidance counselor will then attach a letter of recommendation on your behalf.

Because many high schools have such high student-counselor ratios and there can be a lot of turnover in guidance counseling departments, it is not uncommon for counselors to know very little about the students on whose behalf they are asked to write recommendation letters. Some schools try to solve this by asking teachers to provide short comments on students' performance so that guidance counselors can incorporate these comments into their letters. Here is an example of this type of counselor letter:

> To Whom It May Concern:
>
> I am writing on behalf of Andy McDonald, a senior at John F. Kennedy High School. Because each member of the guidance counseling staff at JFK High School works with over five hundred seniors each year, I have not had the opportunity to get to know Andy very well. However, her teachers have provided excellent

feedback in terms of her work ethic and leadership. No one has a bad word to say about Andy.

Her eleventh grade honors English teacher writes:
"Andy has consistently been among the top ten students in my class this year. She always comes to the classroom prepared and does nice work on her written assignments."

Andy's tenth grade chemistry teacher writes:
"Sophomore year chemistry is a challenging course, and Andy should be proud of the B+ she received for the year. Though she sometimes struggled with the material, Andy always made sure to ask for help if she needed it. Her exam grades reflected a positive trend and her final exam grade of 86 was in the top quarter for her class."

Andy's eleventh grade American history teacher writes:
"Andy was one of the most engaged students in my class. I also worked with her as the faculty adviser to the Young Democrats Club and can speak to her outstanding leadership abilities. Andy was always conscientious about holding meetings and organizing canvassing field trips for our recent congressional elections."

After meeting with Andy to discuss her college plans, I strongly support her application for admission. If you have any questions, please do not hesitate to call me.

Sincerely,
Mr. Smith

While the letter above isn't bad (I've seen much worse), it doesn't really stand out in a sea of thousands of letters that compile short teachers' quotes. If you are wondering if your own guidance counselor might write a similarly boilerplate letter, now is the time to take action.

The first thing to do is to set up a meeting with your counselor, who will have no way to get to know you if you don't spend time together. Be sure to complete your accomplishments doc and bring it to the meeting along with some notes about what makes you special. Have you had any obstacles or challenges—like parents' divorce, a death in the family, or personal health problems—that have contributed to some of your lower grades? If so, you'll also want to share this with your guidance counselor—in fact, the guidance counselor letter is the ideal place to discuss these mitigating circumstances. If your life is relatively obstacle-free, you should still make a list of things that make you a good candidate for college. Are you a frequent contributor to class discussion? Do you love to supplement your classroom learning with visits to museums or by working on behalf of certain causes? What can you give to a college, if accepted? How will you take advantage of this opportunity? A strong guidance counselor letter addresses these types of questions.

When dealing with your guidance counselors, a good rule of thumb is to treat them like they are doing you a favor. Yes, it is technically their job to write you a letter of recommendation, but it is not necessarily their job to write you a good, detailed letter. Be respectful of their time, come prepared to meetings, bring a copy of your accomplishments doc and notes about what makes you special so that they have something in writing. And don't forget to thank them for taking the time to help you get into the college of your dreams.

TIPS FOR COMMUNICATING WITH YOUR COUNSELOR

- Set up a meeting (or several meetings) to introduce yourself.
- Prepare for the meeting with a clear list of questions.
- Complete your accomplishments doc in advance and leave it with your counselor so that she has this information in writing.
- Provide your counselor with written notes about the specific things that make you a unique applicant. These will help your guidance counselor write a more detailed recommendation on your behalf.
- Be sure to discuss any relevant mitigating circumstances that have affected your academics.
- If you have a first-choice school, share this with your counselor; she may want to note this in the recommendation letter.
- Treat your counselor as if she is doing you a favor by going to bat for you.

TEACHER RECOMMENDATIONS

Most selective colleges require at least one teacher recommendation, and some require two. People who have never read college applications might be surprised by just how much the teacher recommendation can sway admissions decisions. Yes, almost all teachers write "good" recommendations in the sense that the letters are positive and complimentary. But when you read hundreds or thousands of letters, you start to get a feel for the teachers who are truly enthusiastic and supportive as compared to the teachers who seem as if they are just going through the motions. Less than perfect students stand to gain the most from teacher raves, especially if their grades are not representative of their intellectual or academic abilities.

The purpose of the teacher recommendation is to understand more about the applicant in an academic context. A great letter describes the student in the classroom—how Brianna takes it upon herself to do outside reading on a topic that interests her; how Scott's valuable contributions to class discussions demonstrate his critical thinking abilities; how that paper Felice wrote about the similarities between post-Communist Russia and present-day China was one of the most insightful in the class. These details give admissions officers a sense of how you'll interact with other students, something that is not captured by the letters or numbers on your transcript.

Like guidance counselors, teachers also have to fill out recommendation forms to answer some questions about the applicant before they attach the letters. On the common application, teachers are asked to rank students in each of the following categories:

- Academic achievement
- Intellectual promise
- Quality of writing
- Creative, original thought
- Productive class discussion
- Respect accorded by faculty
- Disciplined work habits
- Maturity

- Motivation
- Leadership
- Integrity
- Reaction to setbacks
- Concern for others
- Self-confidence
- Initiative, independence
- OVERALL

Using the following scale:
- Below Average
- Average
- Good
- Very Good (well above average)
- Excellent (top 10 percent)
- Outstanding (top 5 percent)
- One of the top few I've encountered in my career

Notice how the first few categories are things like *academic achievement* and *intellectual promise.* Colleges look to your teachers to tell them more about how you are as a student first and a person second. When considering which teacher you want to ask for a recommendation, think about this checklist and ask yourself, *Who is most likely to give me a high ranking? Who have I impressed academically?*

You don't necessarily need to pick the teacher who gave you the highest grade to write your recommendation. Perhaps that B- you got in honors chemistry doesn't tell the whole story of how you consistently improved, did extra credit whenever you could, and made significant contributions to class discussion. Remember, you want each component of your application to *add* something to the admissions officer's impression of who you are and how you'll contribute to a college. When asking for recommendations, pick teachers who know you well and can contribute something to your narrative.

Here are two paragraphs from different teacher recommendations. Can you tell which one is stronger and why?

In my decade of teaching, I can remember few other students who I looked forward to seeing as much as I did when I taught Erin. Erin is fearless; she was always the first to volunteer for an oral presentation or to read aloud from an assignment. Even if Erin didn't have the perfect pronunciation the first time around, she never shied away from a challenge or gave up when she made a mistake. She embraced the journey, and her enthusiasm was contagious. Erin was a real asset to the class.

Precalculus is a very difficult course at Lyndon Johnson High School. Brian received a B for the year and an 88 on the final, which put him on the border of a B+. Brian rarely missed class and completed his assignments on time. He was able to comprehend the material, as he did not receive any grades below 80. Brian is also involved with several activities outside of school, including track and band. He is a well-rounded individual who will do well at any college that accepts him. I offer Brian my highest recommendation.

If you sensed that the first letter is stronger, you're right. Both letters are positive, but the first really describes how Erin contributed to the classroom and gives us a sense of who she is. She's not perfect, but she's an enthusiastic and fearless learner, someone who the teacher looked forward to having in class. Brian's letter doesn't say anything that admissions officers can't learn about him elsewhere in his application—they already know the grade he got because they have his transcript and they know from his activity list that he runs track and plays the saxophone in the marching band. The second letter doesn't add anything to Brian's application.

Now that you understand what makes a good letter, how can you help make your teacher recommendation stand out if you're not the one writing it? I like to encourage students to prepare some materials for their teachers that might help them write stronger letters. Go back through the assignments you completed for these classes and pull out some of your strongest work or reflect on the lessons that you most enjoyed. Then draft a *letter of request* to the teacher(s) who you are asking to write your recommendation(s). In it, thank them for writing your recommendation and highlight some of the things that made you stand out in the classroom. Here's a sample:

Dear Mrs. Goodman,

Thank you for a great year of English and for taking your time to write my letter of recommendation. Now that I have some time to reflect on my experience in your class, I wanted to share some of my thoughts with you.

Once I fully understood the material, I really enjoyed reading the American literature you assigned. The Great Gatsby and Of Mice and Men have become two of my all-time favorite books because they illustrate the beauty of American social mobility and made me want to find a way to work toward achieving greater equality in our society. In addition, after grappling with the challenging works of e. e. cummings, Sylvia Plath, and T. S. Eliot, I learned how to appreciate these poems for their timeless themes. It is amazing to me that these authors had the ability to express themselves in a way that has moved generations of readers. Once I felt confident with the material, I would often help some of my fellow classmates in homeroom, which gave me the opportunity to reread the texts and gain a new appreciation for different words and phrases. I know that I want to take some literature courses in college because I find the material so interesting.

When looking back on where I started, I feel that I improved tremendously as a writer during my time in your class. By incorporating your comments on syntax and organization, I saw my essays become more concise and powerful (especially that paper on Eliot's two poems). I also learned how to use more vivid examples to back up my arguments and the proper use of the subjunctive, which has helped me with everything from standardized tests to the essay I am about to write for my applications. I cherish the comment you wrote on my final research paper, "You have produced an original analysis that contributes *to our understanding of Sylvia Plath's work. You're on your way to becoming a true scholar!"*

    Thank you for being such a great teacher. Also, thank you for taking your time to write my college recommendation letter.

Sincerely,
Christy Smith

The letter above accomplishes two things. First, the student thanks her teacher for agreeing to write the recommendation on her behalf (remember, this isn't actually part of your teacher's job description). She shows her appreciation by describing some of the things she learned and enjoyed. In the process, she also uses specific examples that the teacher may want to include in her recommendation letter, such as the fact that she helped other students with assignments during homeroom or that flattering quote from the final research paper.

TIPS FOR COMMUNICATING WITH YOUR TEACHERS ABOUT RECOMMENDATIONS

- Ask at least *four weeks in advance of the deadline.*
- Provide your teacher with a full list of colleges to which you are applying and the deadlines for recommendation letters.
- Communicate the *specific* ways that you contributed to the class (insightful comments, helping other students, frequently volunteering to participate, taking on extra credit, and so on).
- Share the topics you learned that you genuinely enjoyed in the teacher's class. (If you did outside reading that was inspired by the class, be sure to mention that.)
- Discuss how you think the class has prepared you for college.
- Write a thank-you note!

SUPPLEMENTARY RECOMMENDATIONS

Students who are involved in activities like athletics or service may be wondering if they should send letters of recommendation from their coaches or clergypersons. In my experience, these letters usually aren't necessary unless you have excelled in a certain area. If you've done something that you feel is not adequately expressed in the rest of your application—for example, you led your soccer team to the state championship or started a food drive in your hometown—then a supplementary letter from a supervising adult might add something to your file. As with the other components of your application, the purpose of supplementary recommendations should be to *add* to the admissions officer's understanding of who you are and how you will contribute to the college.

You might have a neighbor or family friend who graduated from one of the colleges on your list and offered to write you an alumni letter of support. These types of letters may help a bit in terms of showing admissions officers that you are interested enough in their college to go out and discuss the school with a graduate that you know. Don't go overboard, however. One or two letters is enough to show your interest. Bombarding admissions officers with extra letters may start to look a little desperate—and don't forget that no one likes to deal with unnecessary paperwork.

SUPPLEMENTARY MATERIALS

Students who are passionate and have invested a significant amount of time in a particular extracurricular activity may decide to submit supplementary materials such as an art portfolio or a musical recording. Each college has a different policy regarding supplementary materials, but most schools will accept them. Because admissions officers aren't experts in things like video production or photography, they typically send these items to the various academic departments at the college for an evaluation.

Naturally, a positive evaluation will work in your favor. But you might be surprised to learn that a neutral or negative evaluation won't generally hurt you if you have other things to offer. A student who is likely to be admitted based on grades, test scores, leadership, and so on won't be rejected because the photography department didn't like his portfolio. However, a borderline student might get a boost from a glowing assessment of her painting or the abstract she sent describing the science research she did over the summer.

If you're considering submitting a recording or portfolio, it's wise to get some feedback from an expert before you send it. Start with your art or music teacher as he probably has a good deal of experience advising students on how to put together portfolios or recordings. Some colleges are very specific in terms of what they want—a recording of no more than five minutes or a portfolio of no fewer than ten images. Some require that you send all materials to the admissions office while others want them sent directly to the academic department that will be evaluating them. When in doubt, call the college and ask about their procedures and deadlines.

INTERVIEWS

When scheduling your campus visit itinerary, it's always a good idea to check if the college that you'll be visiting offers on-campus interviews. While these are by no means required, some colleges—particularly the smaller liberal arts schools—do recommend that students come to campus for an interview. Even if the interview isn't officially recommended, it is another great way for you to demonstrate enthusiasm about the school, which can help you stand out in the applicant pool and possibly compensate for any weaknesses in your transcript or test scores. Colleges that offer on-campus interviews will have information about scheduling them on their websites. If you're planning to visit during an especially popular time like winter or spring break, try to reserve your interview slot as early as possible, because many colleges will get overbooked during high school holidays.

The good news about the college interview is that it is pretty short—usually half an hour—and almost always a positive experience. Your interviewer will either be a member of the admissions staff or an upperclassman who has been hired and trained by the admissions office. She will ask you questions and take notes that will become part of your application. At the same time, your interviewer is also trying to sell you on the school, so it is by no means a hostile encounter packed with "gotcha!" questions.

If you prepare for your on-campus interviews using the tips in this chapter, you'll also be prepared for your alumni interviews as well. Alumni interviews are typically offered after you submit your application to a particular college. A local graduate of that school will then contact you and invite you to meet at a mutually convenient local location, like a Starbucks, the public library, or sometimes her home or office. Alumni interviews pretty much follow the same format as on-campus interviews—they last about half an hour and are seen as two-way exchanges where a representative of the college seeks to learn more about you and you have the opportunity to ask questions about the college. Alumni interviews aren't usually a big factor in admissions decisions, but it never hurts to make a good impression and have one more positive piece of paper in your file. Like on-campus interviews, having an alumni interview is also another opportunity for you to demonstrate your interest in the college.

Whether your interview is on campus or off, as the date approaches, you might be stressing over what to wear. I think most students err on the side of being too dressed up—no need for jackets, ties, or anything resembling a business suit. If you're male, think khakis and a nice button-down or polo shirt. Females can wear a blouse with slacks or a skirt, or they can opt for a casual dress. For shoes, pretty much anything besides sandals, flip-flops, or sneakers will work. Keep it simple and comfortable. You want your interviewer to remember *you*, not what you wore.

TEN STEPS TO A SUCCESSFUL CAMPUS INTERVIEW

Having personally conducted scores of admissions interviews, I have come up with ten easy steps for students who want to kick butt on their college interviews.

1. **Bring your accomplishments doc.** Earlier in this chapter, I go into more detail about how to compose a document that artfully summarizes your extracurricular life. If you have time, it's a great idea to work on your accomplishments doc before your interview so that you can bring it with you and share it with your interviewer. In my experience, many interviewers will use

this as a guide for the rest of the interview and focus their questions about the things on your accomplishments doc. This is a huge plus because you'll be talking about things that you do all the time and the half hour will likely fly by.

2. **Brush up on the big headlines.** If current events aren't your thing, make sure that you start reading a national newspaper like the *New York Times* or the *Wall Street Journal* or watching a reputable newscast (the nightly national newscast on any of the major networks or PBS) a few days before your interview. You can also listen to *All Things Considered* on NPR, either when it is broadcast on the radio or on the exceptionally convenient daily podcast. You don't have to be an expert on every detail of the president's foreign policy agenda, but you should be familiar with the major national and international headlines in case your interviewer brings up current events.

3. **Have a favorite book that was not assigned in school.** With sports, volunteer work, school assignments, standardized test prep, and a social life, it can be hard to find time to read "for fun." That's why interviewers love to ask questions about nonrequired books; your answer can reveal a lot about your intellectual curiosity, especially as a student whose transcript may not reflect the full extent of your brain power. If you can't remember the last time you read a book that was not assigned, browse the *New York Times* bestseller list for reading inspiration when you are in the bookstore or library. If novels aren't your thing, you can always go for a biography of someone you admire or a nonfiction book about a subject that interests you. You'll receive extra points if you avoid clichés like *Harry Potter, Twilight,* or *The Hunger Games.*

4. **Prepare to talk about your favorite subject in high school and what you might want to study at the college.** Some students will find it easy to rave about their favorite high school class and enthusiastically elaborate their future plans for lifelong study of a certain subject. Others will shrug their shoulders and say something like "I guess I like my math class best" when asked about their favorite part of their school day. Ideally, you want to be closer

to the former than the latter. If you're more interested in subjects that aren't typically offered in high school—philosophy, psychology, economics, and so on—that's great; just make sure that you can convey knowledge about these subjects and excitement when you talk about them.

5. **Come up with some examples of interesting things that you do outside of school.** These can be formal extracurricular activities like writing for the school paper or playing offense for the varsity basketball team. They can also be informal pursuits like blogging, photography, or designing your own clothes. Whatever you like to do, be sure that you can talk about why you enjoy it, what you've learned, and how you might like to continue the activity in college, if appropriate.

6. **Find an issue or cause that you care about.** Colleges want students who will use their education to make a difference in the world, which is why many interviewers will ask you to talk about an issue or cause that means something to you. If you're not an "activist," you can still give a thoughtful answer to this question. To prepare for your interview, consider the injustices that you have encountered or read about that you wish you could solve. You can talk about anything from saving the environment to raising money for autism research as long as you show that you care about things that don't just affect you personally and that you want to make a positive impact in the world around you.

7. **Learn about the college.** Any time you have an interview, it's important to be familiar with the organization that you are hoping to join. Unfortunately, most college websites offer only the most superficial information about the school. A much better source of information is the campus newspaper, which you can easily find online. Browse through the articles, and you'll get a sense of the major issues on campus. The opinion pages are also a great way to access unfiltered student voices.

8. **Be ready to ask your interviewer three questions.** Most students don't realize that interviews are a two-way exchange; a representative from college is there to learn more about you, and you

are there to learn more about the college. You'll find that every interview usually ends with "Do you have any questions for me?" Come prepared with three questions for the interviewer to show your curiosity and thoughtfulness. Avoid "brochure" questions like "What is your student-faculty ratio?" (You can easily get this information from the college's website.) Instead, opt for more qualitative questions like "Can you please tell me more about the unusual freshman orientation program?" You could also use the knowledge you gain from reading the school newspaper to ask about a specific issue such as "Where will student organizations be able to meet during the two-year renovation of the student center?"

9. **Write a thank-you note on paper.** Your interviewer might receive hundreds of emails a day and only a handful of written notes each week. As a student who wants to put your best foot forward, go the extra mile to make an impression by sending a handwritten thank-you note. The note can be simple. Mention how you enjoyed meeting the interviewer and include one or two details from your conversation. Don't forget to sign the note with your name, email address, and telephone number just in case she wants to keep in touch with you.

10. **Practice, practice, practice.** If you're like most students reading this book, chances are you've never actually been interviewed for anything before. The good news is that interviewing is a skill that you can learn through practice. Having personally conducted scores of interviews as a former admissions officer, I've included lots of sample college interview questions below so that you can do just that. Give them to your parents or someone else you trust and instruct them to ask you a few at a time. Try to space out your preparation—practice a couple of questions over breakfast or dinner, or in the car. I find that it's best not to "cram" for an interview because students can become overwhelmed by too many unfamiliar questions. You might not feel completely comfortable answering all of these questions the first time, but you'll quickly see improvements with some practice.

COLLEGE INTERVIEW QUESTIONS
TO PRACTICE AT HOME

QUESTIONS ABOUT YOURSELF

- Tell me about yourself.
- Tell me about your family.
- Tell me about the town you live in.
- How do you think your teachers would describe you?
- How do you think your friends would describe you?
- Tell me about a time that you participated in a group project.
- Would you describe yourself as a leader or a team player? Can you give me an example of how you embody this trait?
- What inspires you?
- What would you do with a free afternoon?
- When was the last time you visited a museum?
- What's your favorite movie? Television show?
- If your life were a movie, who would play you and what would be the major plot line?

QUESTIONS ABOUT ACADEMICS OR CURRENT EVENTS

- Tell me about your high school.
- Who is your favorite teacher and why?
- What is your favorite class and why?
- If you could change one thing about your high school, what would it be?
- What is the best thing about being a student at your high school? What is the worst?
- What is the best book you read for fun in the past year? Can you tell me why you liked it?
- What was the last thing you read in the newspaper?
- Name some magazines or websites that you read regularly.
- If you could change anything about the world, what would it be?
- Tell me about an issue that matters to you and why.

QUESTIONS ABOUT CHALLENGES AND OBSTACLES

- What is the most difficult book you have ever read? How did it challenge you?
- What is the hardest class you are taking this year? How are you coping with the stress?
- Have you ever had a disagreement with a teacher? If so, what did you do?
- What is the biggest obstacle you have ever faced and how did you overcome it?
- What would you say is your greatest weakness?
- What's the biggest mistake you have ever made?

QUESTIONS ABOUT EXTRACURRICULAR INVOLVEMENT

- Are you involved in any extracurricular activities or clubs?
- What opportunities have you taken to be a leader outside of school?
- Do you work? If so, please tell me about your job.
- What accomplishment are you most proud of?

QUESTIONS ABOUT GOING TO COLLEGE

- Why do you want to go to college?
- What do you think you want to study in college?
- Why do you want to go to this college?
- How do you think you can contribute to this college?

CHAPTER 7 ACTION STEPS

❑ Start working on your college applications the summer before senior year. Give them the time and respect that they deserve.

❑ If you do a lot outside of school, create an outstanding, easy-to-read accomplishments doc.

❑ Review your high school profile to understand how your academics stack up against those of your classmates.

❑ Advocate for yourself when it comes to recommendations! Follow the tips in this chapter for communicating with counselors and teachers.

❑ Follow the ten steps for interview preparation and practice questions at home.

CHAPTER 8

WRITING YOUR COLLEGE ESSAY

By the time senior year rolls around, there's not much you can do about your grades. However, there are plenty of things you can do to boost your chances of admission to the college of your dreams and to put together the best possible application. Writing an outstanding college essay is a terrific opportunity to show the admissions committee something about yourself and what makes you special. The problem is that most high school students have no experience writing about themselves and aren't sure what makes an essay stand out. This chapter walks you through the essay-writing process, shows you some common essay mistakes, and gives you samples of real essays that worked.

One of the first things I do whenever I work with a high school senior is help the student understand how the Common Application is read by admissions officers. Typically, the application materials are read in the following order: personal and family information, extracurricular activities, essays, transcript, scores, counselor recommendation, teacher recommendation(s), interview (if any), and then any supplementary materials. Interestingly, your essays are often looked at before your transcript. This allows you to introduce yourself before the person reading your application gets to the numbers and letters that make up your GPA. You know how the right lighting in a photograph can make a person look fresh and attractive and the wrong lighting can make the same person look old and tired, right? When it comes to the college essay, students should think of themselves as lighting designers setting the mood. You want to create an atmosphere that will make those Bs look as attractive as possible.

THE FIVE FOOLPROOF RULES OF ESSAY WRITING

I'm not going to lie to you; writing a great college essay takes work. You have to be willing to show your essay to impartial readers (your parents might have something useful to say, but they shouldn't be the only adults giving you feedback) and to rewrite something that doesn't work until you get it right. Use the resources at your disposal—your guidance counselor, English teacher, smart friends and neighbors. Give yourself enough time to get feedback and take it in. And remember, nothing that you have ever enjoyed reading was a first draft. Professional writers know better than anyone that the only way to write something worthwhile is to work on it (and work on it, and work on it).

Are you ready to get on the road to college essay greatness? Here are five rules to help you get your creative juices flowing, identify good ideas, and make them sing on paper. By following these rules, you'll have no trouble writing something heartfelt and genuine that truly stands out in a sea of college essays about family vacations and soccer games.

1. The essay must add something to your application.
2. Don't bite off more than you can chew in five hundred words.
3. Show, don't tell.

4. Grab your reader in the first paragraph.
5. Mark your territory.

RULE 1: THE ESSAY MUST ADD
SOMETHING TO YOUR APPLICATION

The admissions office will be getting lots of information about you from your transcript, test scores, and activities, but the personal essay is a unique space to show your voice. Use these precious pages to tell the admissions office something that they would not otherwise know by reading the rest of your application. Many students choose a "safe" topic about an extracurricular activity like "Why Mock Trial Matters to Me" or "How I Scored the Winning Touchdown." This is a bad idea. Look at the Common Application, and you'll see that the admissions officers will view your activities list before they read your essays. They already know that you like Mock Trial or that you play football because these things are listed on your application. Unless you're answering a question that expressly asks you to write about an extracurricular activity, stay away from focusing solely on things that are already on your resume. These kinds of topics usually feel redundant—and because so many students write about activities, these essays rarely stand out.

You are probably wondering nervously, *If I can't write an essay about my activities, what on earth am I going to write about?* Some of the best essays are actually about observations and experiences that may have seemed inconsequential at the time but show a good deal about you. In one of my all-time favorite essays, a student named James wrote about how he volunteered to show the "new guy" at school around when he was in sixth grade. James did a fantastic job of setting the scene, making jokes about middle school, and being honest about the fact that, although he and the "new guy" always had a connection, they didn't become best friends by the time they got to high school. By telling a casual story and drawing readers in with personal details and showing them how he interpreted the world, James was able to show the admissions committee something that they would have no other way of knowing—that he is a *genuinely* friendly and warm person: the type of person you'd want to show you around if you were new at school, the type of person you'd want as your roommate, the type of person professors would want in their classes. No wonder he got accepted to his first-choice school.

Because James's story and others like it happen all the time, it can be tough for students to recognize when an event is worth exploring in an essay. Sally Rubenstone, a college admissions expert who writes the must-read "Ask the Dean" column on the popular College Confidential website (www.collegeconfidential.com/dean), has a great list of questions that she uses to help her students think of possible under-the-radar essay gems like James's story. Answering these questions will help you take a step back and consider the wide range of things that make you unique and interesting. Grab a pencil and piece of paper and start writing the first thing that pops into your head.

- What single achievement are you most proud of?
- What makes your family different from other families?
- What's the most difficult thing you've had to do in your life?
- What do you do better than almost anyone else?
- What's the nicest thing you've ever done for anyone? (Name a few, if several come to mind.)
- What do you think your teachers say about you when you're not around?
- What do you think your friends say about you when you're not around?
- What do you worry about most (besides college admissions, of course!)?
- What really makes you laugh?
- What's your all-time favorite book and why?
- What are your favorite foods? What foods do you avoid (or even spit out)?
- Do you have a favorite object or item of clothing?
- What's your favorite bumper-sticker slogan (real or imagined)?
- Where do you think you will be and what will you be doing ten years from now?

- If you could do one thing over in your life, what would it be and why?
- If a highly selective college had to pick between you and one other applicant, why should it pick you? (Feel free to make a list of five or ten reasons why they should take you and not the other candidate. Be both serious and funny, if you can.)

Take a look at what you wrote. Did you find yourself continuously going back to particular characteristics, like how funny you are or how you inspire other people when you get excited about something? Do any of the stories you jotted down seem particularly salient? The right topic should feel easy to write about because you have so much to say about it, and because it truly captures something about you.

RULE 2: DON'T BITE OFF MORE THAN YOU CAN CHEW IN FIVE HUNDRED WORDS

Now that you have a general idea of what you might like to write about, you need to understand how to express the idea in a compelling five hundred words. Many students feel paralyzed by the college essay because they have no idea how they can summarize their whole lives in just four or five paragraphs. The answer is simple: you can't do it, so don't try. Not even Ernest Hemingway, who was known as the master of brevity in storytelling, could tell someone's complete life story in five hundred words. Instead of trying to cover everything, focus on a particular event or experience that illustrates a bigger theme. James's brief stint as a middle-school tour guide is a perfect example. By telling this particular story, he also tells us something meaningful about who he is as a person.

Every time I think about the importance of rule #2, I am always reminded of a student I met while volunteering at the International High School at Lafayette, a New York City charter school for recent immigrants. For the most part, it was easy to help this group of students with their college essays because they had such fascinating, diverse backgrounds—they were brought together from places as different as Poland and Pakistan. After several meetings with students who wrote about aspects of their immigration experiences or the challenges of trying to integrate into an unfamiliar society, a shy Uzbeki student handed me his handwritten college essay. Almost every sentence started with the words "I am." *I am strong and determined. I am quiet when I meet new people but have many close friends. I am one of the best soccer players in my class.* It was more like a list of personal qualities than a cohesive college essay with a narrative. I asked him if he understood the purpose of the college essay.

When he answered, "To tell the people at the college who I am," I couldn't help but smile. He was expressing a literal interpretation of something I have seen many students try to do. If you approach the assignment as trying to tell your life story in five hundred words, you'll end up with a disjointed list of personal qualities instead of an actual essay. The good news is that students who are intimidated by the task of summing up their entire lives in a few paragraphs can relax. There is a difference between telling someone who you are and telling a story that shows something about you. Your job is simpler than it sounds—tell a good story. Once the Uzbeki student understood the purpose of the assignment, he was able to write a compelling essay about the challenges of going to an American high school without knowing the language and how he was eventually able to learn English.

RULE 3: SHOW, DON'T TELL

"Show, don't tell" is one of the biggest clichés of high school English classes, but it has been repeated so many times because it is true. Think about the student from Uzbekistan. Ironically, writing a list of I am's doesn't actually tell the reader very much about the student at all. Anyone can write "I am brave," but only a unique individual could tell a story about how she risked a bad grade in math by enrolling in the hardest class in school or how she stood up to a bully. The students who tell these types of stories well won't have to write sentences like "I am brave." Their stories already convey this to the reader. If you do this, you will earn the trust of readers by pulling them into your world and showing them a part of who you are.

What's the difference between showing and telling? When you "show," you add descriptions that allow readers to identify with you, to relate to you and your experiences. You give them details that enable them to picture a scene in front of them, like they are watching a scene from a movie. Let me share some examples so that you can see exactly what I mean.

> **Tell:** I am tired.
>
> **Show:** All day long, I walk around in a daze, forcing my eyes to stay open until the blissful moment when my head hits the pillow and I can finally give in to my mind-numbing exhaustion.

> **Tell:** I am happy.
>
> **Show:** I jump up and down, squealing the way I did when my parents surprised me on my fifth birthday with the doll that I had been lusting after for months.

> **Tell:** I am nervous.
>
> **Show:** My heart beats so loudly that I wonder if the microphone pinned to my shirt will broadcast the thumping to the audience.

You get the picture, right? In each of these "show" examples, the reader has the opportunity to come along on the writer's journey of being tired, happy, or nervous. We are able to identify with these emotions and understand how the writer experiences them. Every good writer needs to follow the "show, don't tell" rule, but as a student with some flaws on your transcript, it is especially important that you make a connection with the person reading your application and communicate the essence of you that isn't captured on your two-dimensional transcript.

Now that you know what "showing" looks like in general, I want to give you an example of how it can improve your essay. This paragraph was written by a student named Brie, who was known in her family as the go-to person for puzzles and word games. She was a whiz at the *New York Times* crossword and could put together a Rubik's Cube like a champ. For her college essay, Brie could have written something like "I love puzzles, word games, and problem-solving subjects like math and physics." But sentences like that make readers fall asleep. It was a good thing that Brie was smart enough to show her readers how her love of problem solving seeped into her everyday life. She opened her essay on her love of puzzle solving with the following scene:

> *Eight duffel bags, seven pairs of skis, seven boot bags, and a trunk space of four by five feet. Wondering why we packed so much for a three-day trip, I size up the items and line the four largest duffel bags on the floor of the trunk. Next I wedge the hard boot bags in the crevices and then stack the smaller duffels on top as the trunk starts to resemble the jammed-packed bookshelf in our basement. The skis, which I carefully balance on the tops of the headrests, become the bookends. Soon, the Sussman family is off to New Hampshire. As excited as I am about the ski trip, I am even more fulfilled by solving this life-sized puzzle.*

Brie nails the "show, don't tell" rule. In about one hundred words, she pulls us in and makes us trust her as a narrator. By using descriptive details about her plan of attack, she makes us feel as if we are there with her as she packs up the car. We see how her mind works, how she fits the boots and skis together like a puzzle. We experience her satisfaction as she completes the challenge. Most importantly, we feel that we know something about her—and we want to learn more.

RULE 4: GRAB YOUR READER IN THE FIRST PARAGRAPH

Admissions officers read about thirty applications a day, which adds up to thousands of college essays each year. This is why you hear so much advice about the need to make your essay stand out among a sea of other qualified high school students, especially the ones whose grades and SAT scores might be a little better than yours. One of the best ways to grab your reader is to start with a scene like Brie's. The scene doesn't have to be dramatic. It can be anything active—how the melon feels in your hands when you're selecting the best produce at the supermarket, the sound of the leaves crunching under your shoes when you walk to your best friend's house, what the grains of sugar look like when they dissolve in your coffee. Just using active language, set in the present, is often enough to draw readers into a specific time and place. If you look through the opening sentences of some influential novels, you'll see that great writers use this tactic too:

> "Mrs. Dalloway said she would buy the flowers herself." (Virginia Woolf, *Mrs. Dalloway*)

> "It was a queer, sultry summer, the summer they electrocuted the Rosenbergs, and I didn't know what I was doing in New York." (Sylvia Plath, *The Bell Jar*)

> "Stately, plump Buck Mulligan came from the stairhead, bearing a bowl of lather on which a mirror and a razor lay crossed." (James Joyce, *Ulysses*)

Starting with a scene is a great way to grab your readers and pull them in. We can't help but wonder whether it is unusual for Mrs. Dalloway to buy her own flowers, why Sylvia Plath's narrator is confused about the fact that she is in New York, and who will get a shave from Buck Mulligan. One of my favorite college essays was about a student's lifelong obsession with historic soap operas and especially the Tudor dynasty of England. (You may remember Henry VIII killing his wives from history class or perhaps from the Showtime series about the Tudors.) The writer, a young woman named Maya, opened with a scene from her life in which she is engrossed in Tudor drama:

> *I am seven. My best friend, Tammy, and I are play-acting with our Princess Barbie dolls. However, it isn't the Barbies that I'm interested in. What I really want to do is act out some thrilling intrigues of the Tudor court, be it Elizabeth I's victory over the Spanish Armada or Mary Tudor's life under the authority of her "evil" stepmother—Anne Boleyn.*

The scene from Maya's childhood pulls us in and makes us want to learn more about her and her quirky interest in the Tudors. Maya's introduction also works so well because she is authentic. While there are plenty of other students who might enjoy history, they could not tell that exact story in the same way Maya does.

RULE 5: MARK YOUR TERRITORY

To "mark your territory," you must submit an essay that could only be written by one person—and that one person is you. Though the importance of marking your territory may seem obvious, it is actually very challenging for most students who are new to writing personal essays. Let's take a common essay topic, like playing on a basketball team, for example. Take a moment to read the essay below and make a note of the places where the writer marks his territory with words or sentences that could only be written by a specific individual.

> *I love sports and I have found that there is nothing like being part of a team. I played basketball for the town of Northbrook for ten years. My experience was very special. I was with a group of guys who were not necessarily my friends but with whom I formed a close bond while we were on the court. If a team is going to be successful, they have to support one another for the sake of the whole. I played power forward, which means I had to get rebounds in order to score. When my teammate had the ball, I had to think like him so I would be where he needed me when he passed the ball. I don't hog the ball to get into the spotlight because that is not how a successful team operates. I learned how to sacrifice my own needs for the sake of others.*

Besides some specifics like being from Northbrook, Illinois, and playing power forward, this entire paragraph feels as if it could be written by *anyone* who has ever played team basketball. Most people who play basketball enjoy the sport. They bond with their teammates. Because it is a team sport, it's natural that players feel that the game makes them more aware of others. There's nothing in this paragraph that helps the reader get to know this student. He failed to mark his territory.

Now take a look at another introductory paragraph for an essay about sports by a boy named Josh.

The phone rang inside Room 242 at the rundown Comfort Inn. The constant, shrill sound of the wake-up call succeeded in terminating my peaceful dreams. It was 6:30 a.m. on a Saturday. In only a few hours, the temperature would reach triple digits, just another summer day in Virginia. I went through my morning routine: a cold shower, a mediocre breakfast from the free buffet in the lobby, and twenty minutes of stretching. After three months of intense preparation, today was the day where it was my turn to perform, to stand out among the 250 players from around the country competing for the attention of 100 coaches representing top baseball programs at some of the nation's finest colleges. On the outside, it must have looked like my entire world hinged on the success of this moment, but something inside me was already starting to realize that maybe this wasn't what I wanted to do with my life.

This paragraph works because Josh does a great job of following the rules of college essay writing. He takes a common topic like sports and marks his territory by including details—a rundown Comfort Inn, triple-digit temperature, competing against the country's top 250 baseball players—that show the high stakes of this big day. Then he surprises us with second thoughts about this significant moment. In 150 words, Josh has drawn us into his story while showing us that he is a critical thinker who is willing to question his actions instead of just going with the flow. He makes us want to learn more about him.

How do you know if you have successfully marked your territory? Once you're done with a draft of your essay, ask yourself, *If I dropped this paper on the floor at school and my best friend found it, would she know it was mine even if my name wasn't on it?* If the answer is yes, then you've nailed the task because you have an essay that could only be written by you. You can also recruit a few close friends or relatives to read it. Ask them, "Does this sound like *me*?"

MASTERING THE SHORT COMMON APPLICATION ESSAY

The Common Application has two required essays: a short one-thousand-character paragraph on a meaningful activity and a longer, five-hundred-word personal statement. I recommend dipping your toes into the college essay waters with the short essay because students are usually pretty comfortable writing about one of their activities.

The instructions for the short essay are straightforward: "Please briefly elaborate on one of your extracurricular activities or work experiences in the space below." Because this essay prompt asks you to write about an activity, there will be some overlap between the topic you choose and your resume. This doesn't, however, mean that you should throw rule #1 out the window. You must still write something that adds to your application, not just list your soccer awards or the basic responsibilities of your part-time job. What did you learn from this activity? How did it challenge you? How will this experience help you contribute to college life?

Noah's essay about Quiz Bowl does a great job of illustrating his thirst for knowledge (and his sense of humor):

> Having been a bit nerdy most of my life, as a freshman in high school, I had no desire to join Quiz Bowl and participate in perpetuating a stereotype. But it was as if Quiz Bowl was a supernatural force pulling me into its orbit; after a misunderstanding in finding a Debate Club meeting, I ended up at the Quiz Bowl tryouts—it was meant to be. In Quiz Bowl, it matters that I know about Iditarod dogsled racing or that I can recall specific Mao Tsetung quotes. After a few years on the team, I appeared on The Challenge, a televised quiz show between regional high schools. It was thrilling to have dozens of fans (it was local TV) watching me do something I love. Beyond the glory that Quiz Bowl has brought me, the most rewarding aspect has also been the most unexpected one. Quiz Bowl's gravitational pull attracts people from all groups: artists, athletes, musicians, and people who defy stereotypes. This, I believe, is what makes Quiz Bowl so special.

Noah manages to pack a lot into these one thousand characters—in just one paragraph, he shows us that he's smart, funny, and values having friends from different cliques.

When you sit down to write your short essay, you might be surprised at how difficult it can be to say something meaningful in a limited space. The best thing to do is to forget about the length requirements in your first draft. Start by writing everything that you want to say about this activity and what you've learned from it. Allow yourself to explore and establish your voice. Once your point of view is clear, you can edit and trim the text.

WRITING A KILLER COMMON APPLICATION PERSONAL STATEMENT

After you finish writing your short Common Application essay, you'll be ready to tackle the more intimidating five-hundred-word personal statement. An endless variety of subjects will be appropriate for this essay as long as what you write adds something to your application and shows the admissions office what you have to offer. Certain topics, however, can be somewhat difficult to pull off because they are so commonly used by high school students. If you want to write about one of these, you need to be extra creative to make your essay stand out. Here are some topics that you might want to think twice about:

- **Family vacations.** Admissions officers aren't exactly rolling in dough, so you risk making your reader jealous if you write about a fancy family vacation. Besides, this topic makes it difficult to show something distinctive about yourself besides having generous parents who take you to cool places. These essays tend to blend together.
- **Hot-button topics/religion.** You don't know the people who will be reading your application. While it's important to express your opinions, controversial or religious topics—things like abortion, gay marriage, school prayer, and political affiliations—can alienate a reader. If you do choose a hot-button topic,

present yourself as a reasonable person who respects different points of view. Admissions officers want students who can get along with others.

- **How I saved the day/scored the goal/won the race.** College applicants want to impress, which explains why so many write essays featuring themselves as the hero or heroine saving the day. These typically start out with an obstacle—the big game, a campaign for class president, starting a difficult hike—then the writer elaborates on his self-doubt over completing the challenging task and (surprise!) ends with victory. Be proud of your accomplishments, but don't tell a story full of clichés. Stories about trying something that didn't work out can be just as interesting as predictable heroics, if not more so.

- **Sob stories.** You may be tempted to appeal to a reader's sense of pity by writing about the worst thing that has ever happened to you. The problem is that admissions officers don't admit students that they feel sorry for; they admit students who will contribute something to the college. If you do want to write about something sad or difficult, think about your motivation: are you telling the story to be liked or because it is a definitive story in your life? If it's the latter, go for it by exploring what you learned from this challenge.

- **Writing your college essay.** Every year, plenty of students submit college essays *about* writing their college essays or about the process of applying to college. One of the few things that the admissions office already knows about you is that you are applying to college. Find more interesting things to talk about than how stressed out you are or the limitations of describing yourself in five hundred words. You will be compared with other applicants who are in the same boat but still manage to come up with creative, engaging personal essays that reveal something about themselves.

So how can you produce a killer college essay even if you do write about one of the topics mentioned above? Easy—by following the five rules of essay writing. The following essay was written by Jenny, who has juvenile diabetes. But instead of playing a pity card, Jenny writes about her illness in a way that shows her creativity by playing off her love of mystery novels.

"The pipes, the pipes are calling" boomed through the class-room. As I sang "Oh Danny Boy," I began to sweat, shake, and feel lightheaded. My body—sturdy through grueling soccer practice, through the crash of lacrosse checks, through basket-ball suicide sprints—was no longer under my control. I let out a gurgle before everything went black.

I awoke on the floor with thirty pairs of eyes staring at me.

By the time I got to eighth grade, I thought I was a pro at handling my diabetes. However, that morning, I woke up twenty minutes late for school and ran out the door, oblivious to the granola bar laid out on the table. The day went by as usual until fourth period chorus class. "Danny Boy."

It was around the same time that I discovered my love of mystery novels. My favorite detective, Hercule Poirot, was obsessed with order. He would not eat eggs of different sizes, he groomed his mustache perfectly, and kept his clothing immaculate; Poirot's routines reminded me of my attention to carbs, insulin dosages, and fitness. I related to Poirot's obses-sion with details because I knew I would have to maintain a rigid regimen to prevent another diabetic episode.

On my first day of high school, as always, my mom packed a note in my lunch, tallying the number of carbs in my meal and how much insulin I would need. She gave me my lunch with a look of calm desperation and said that it was time for me to take responsibility and figure out insulin dosages by myself. She reminded me of the characters in Agatha Christie novels who would approach Detective Poirot with the challenge of a mys-tery. It was now up to me to crack the case of my diabetes.

Though I started to take steps toward self-reliance, I wasn't ready to fend for myself. Channeling my inner Detective Poirot, I searched for the perfect person to help, someone with an ency-clopedic knowledge of nutrition to fill the role that my mother had always played. Poirot used his "little gray cells" to find the person he was after; I tried to do the same. My two best friends, Amanda and Rachel, seemed like solid options. Or, maybe I could enlist one of my twenty cousins. I knew I had to make my selection carefully. Poirot was never fooled by the red herring, and he kept searching until he had the answer.

As with the most gripping mystery novels, the evidence I needed was revealed over time. Last year, I was getting lunch with my friends when my blood sugar got low. Amanda somehow managed to retrieve a Coke within seconds. This past sum-mer in Costa Rica, I had no idea how many carbs were in my rice and beans. My cousin Barbara used her basic Spanish to decode the nutrition information on the food bags.

Like Detective Poirot in Murder on the Orient Express, *I soon realized that the answer had always been right in front of me, but I was asking the wrong question. Poirot uses his "little gray cells" to deduce that there was not one culprit, but twelve; and I discovered that all of my friends and family could offer support. I don't have to find one perfect person to fill my mother's shoes nor do I have to fend for myself the rest of my life. I have a team of support; and, if they aren't around, I always have my little gray cells.*

Jenny takes a well-covered topic—struggling with an illness—and writes about it in a way that shows true creativity. Her dramatic first paragraph instantly makes us want to learn more about why she fainted. Instead of telling a predictable story about the challenges of living with a chronic illness, Jenny makes an interesting connection between her beloved mystery novels and her quest to manage her diabetes. She isn't afraid to be vulnerable along the way, and she ends up in a stronger place because of her journey to find support. Using the five rules of essay writing, Jenny has hit a home run. This is a winning Common Application personal statement.

"WHY DO YOU WANT TO GO TO OUR COLLEGE?" AND OTHER SUPPLEMENTARY ESSAYS

Just because there is a Common Application does not mean that you simply fill out one form, write the required essays, and send it off to every college on your list. If only it were that easy! The idea of a Common Application is a bit of a fallacy because many colleges also require additional essays in their supplements. Some colleges ask really specific questions like "What place, people, or culture would you like to get to know better and why?" (Grinnell College) or "If you had a theme song—a piece of music that describes you best—what would it be and why? Please include the name of the song and the artist" (Smith College). Before you start working on your supplementary essays, compile all of the essay questions on one document and see if any of the themes overlap. For example, a student may have a favorite Mexican folk melody and be able to talk about her passion for Mexican culture in both essays. If possible, it is better to spend more time on fewer essays and send them to multiple schools.

Though the particular wording may vary, many schools want students to answer some version of the following question in their supplements: why do you want to go to our college? This essay gauges how serious you are about your application. Have you taken the time to do research about the college? What makes you a good match for this school? How would you take advantage of the opportunities on campus, and how would you give back to the community? Why should the admissions committee take you over other qualified applicants?

Because you don't have a perfect academic record, it is especially important that you invest time in these essays. I can't tell you how many students give essentially the same answer to all the colleges that ask this question. They talk vaguely about the beautiful campus, good reputation, and the location. Here's an example: "After spending time on the beautiful G.W. campus, I know that going to one of the best colleges in Washington, DC, will expose me to many exciting opportunities." None of these details really tells us much about the applicant and why she is a good match for George Washington University in particular.

Your "Why do you want to go here?" essay should start with what you want to study. As a student with a "soft" academic track record, it is especially important to be explicit about your academic goals and your plan to accomplish them. Reference specific professors whose research you admire or classes that you would like to take (avoid courses that every college offers like Psychology 101). Write about your plans to complete a senior thesis or pursue a unique internship opportunity in this area. And, most importantly, don't use generic terms that might apply to other colleges. The key here is to be specific!

After you've outlined the unique academic contributions you hope to make, you can include details about how you plan to spend your time outside of class. Go to the college's directory of student organizations and find specific clubs that you might like to join that tie into the things you've already done in high school. You can also explore completely new activities as long as you say that this is your plan. Just give enough details to show the admissions officers that you have done your research about the unique aspects of their school.

Finally, it is a good idea to show you understand the school's traditions and values. Do they have an honor code that you admire? Are you excited to paint your face in school colors at football games? Are you interested in attending one of the many lecture series on campus? Every school has something that makes it unique, besides courses and clubs. Show the admissions officers that you understand the intangible benefits of belonging to this particular community and that you're someone who can make a contribution, if given the chance. Happy writing!

CHAPTER 8 ACTION STEPS

❏ Follow the five rules of essay writing:
   1. The essay must add something to your application.
   2. Don't bite off more than you can chew in five hundred words.
   3. Show, don't tell.
   4. Grab your reader in the first paragraph.
   5. Mark your territory.

❏ Think twice about the clichéd essay topics.

❏ Don't worry about the word limit in the first draft. Once you have clarified your thoughts and ideas, you can trim the text.

❏ Never be generic with the "Why do you want to go to our college?" essay. Showcase your knowledge of the school and how you can make a unique academic, extracurricular, and social contribution.

CHAPTER 9

GETTING THE RED-CARPET TREATMENT:

STUDENTS WITH SPECIAL CIRCUMSTANCES

If you've ever been to a presentation given by an admissions officer—an on-campus information session, a presentation at your high school, or even a speech at the local library—you know that most people in the audience are there to get more information about a very specific question: can I get into this college? Unfortunately, the audience almost never receives a clear answer. Instead of helping students understand exactly what the admissions committee wants or how it makes decisions, the admissions officers generally talk about a wide range of desirable attributes that might catch their eye—they look at academics *and* personal qualities, for students who are good at many things *and* for applicants who have particular passions, for leaders *and* quiet intellectuals, for legacy students *and* those who are the first in their families to go to college. No wonder it's so hard to understand what colleges want and what your chances are of being accepted. Admissions officers often sound as if they contradict themselves.

The answer to one of the most important questions—can I get into this college?—is different for different types of students. Because of the various institutional priorities just mentioned, certain types of students have an advantage in the admissions process. If you fall into one of these categories, you're in luck! This chapter outlines the different types of students who will get the red-carpet treatment in the admissions office—including athletes, students of statistically underrepresented ethnicities, first-generation college students, legacies, and students with unique talents—and how to make the most of your application if you happen to be part of these groups.

ATHLETES

Athletes get to go to the front of the line in the admissions process. They also have to start visiting and communicating with colleges earlier than other students because many coaches finalize their list of recruited students in the summer before or early during senior year. Although there may be some slight differences among various sports, the basics of the process work the same for most athletes who are trying to get recruited to play on the college level. Andrew Herman, who has spent forty-five years as an athletic director and fifteen years advising students on the recruiting process for student-athletes, worked with me on developing these ten basic steps to get the proverbial ball rolling.

1. BE GOOD AT THE SPORT

What do I mean by this obvious-sounding piece of advice? Most athletes who get recruited aren't just playing their sport in school; they're also playing in camps and tournaments and investing time in off-season training. For most sports, it's also important to begin a weight-training program because college athletes are bigger, faster, and stronger than high school athletes.

2. BECOME FAMILIAR WITH FOUR IMPORTANT LETTERS—NCAA

The National Collegiate Athletic Association is the Walmart of college sports; they basically have everything you need. NCAA teams are divided into three classifications: Divisions I, II, and III. Each of these divisions has different regulations for how and when coaches can communicate with students, so check out the rules for both your sport and division. The NCAA website (www.ncaa.org) also provides a list of colleges with teams for each sport, where those teams are ranked, who coaches those teams, and which coaches win games. Finally, the NCAA is responsible for regulating and for providing information on academic requirements, so review the requirements for your sport. Although the GPA cutoff for most college teams is a 2.0 (a C average), B students need to familiarize themselves with NCAA course and standardized testing requirements to be sure that they meet all the requirements.

3. FIND ROLE MODELS

Because every sport is different in terms of how much outside training is encouraged, it's important to do research about how other student-athletes in your sport got recruited. If you're on a competitive high school team that has sent recruited athletes to colleges in the past, ask your coach for advice or talk to the more senior members of the team who are going through the recruiting process. Some colleges also have athletes' bios online, so do some digging and see if you can spot some themes. Did all the lacrosse players at your top-choice school play for a particular travel team or attend a camp? Did the rowers place in certain high school regattas? Did the gymnasts train at particular gyms? See what the athletes you admire have done to get them where they are.

4. GET A HEAD START

Most athletes commit to a college by the summer before or early in the fall of their senior year. Most coaches begin recruiting athletes in their junior year of high school, especially for spring sports. Since the athletic recruiting process is earlier than the regular college admissions timeline, you should start considering colleges by the end of sophomore year or beginning of junior year. This doesn't mean that you need to run to every college campus you've ever heard of. You can start by putting together a list of potential colleges that might be a good fit for you athletically and academically by doing some research online.

5. GET THE BEST GRADES YOU CAN

Although athletes are favored in the admissions process, you still have to meet the college's minimum GPA and SAT requirements to be accepted. Student-athletes can cast a wide net in the beginning of the process because you still have time to improve as an athlete and a student. It is fine to keep your options open and have a working list of about twenty colleges at this point, even though you will end up applying to fewer schools.

6. CREATE A RESUME TO SEND TO COACHES

Don't wait until coaches track you down and ask you for this resume; take the initiative to send it to coaches at the schools that interest you. A good resume will have the following information:

- Name and contact info
- Relevant physical characteristics (height, weight, and so on)
- Athletic experience (include teams you play for, positions you play, time you spend training, and so on; also put future tournaments and camps that you intend to play in, if relevant)
- Academic experience (basics like GPA and SAT; if you haven't taken the SAT yet, put the future date)

You can also include things like outside hobbies or other extracurricular interests. Don't be afraid to put your own personality in there.

Here's a slightly altered sample of an athletic resume for a squash player who was recruited to some of the most selective liberal arts colleges in the country.

SQUASH

Experience: 2001–present, 10+ hrs/wk; 48 wks/yr

Leadership/Awards

- U.S. Squash Ranking: U19 #39 (January 16, 2012)
- High School Varsity Team Captain, Grades 9, 11, 12
- MVP, Grades 9, 10
- Undefeated Season, Grade 10
- U.S. Squash Scholar Athlete Award, Grade 11

Selected Tournaments

- Junior Championship Tour Tournaments, Grades 9–12 (competed in 4)
- Gold Tournaments, Grades 9–12 (competed in 6)
- Silver Tournaments, Grades 9–12 (competed in 13)
- U.S. Junior Silver Championships, Grades 9–11 (competed in 2)
- U.S. Junior Bronze Squash Championships, Grades 9–11 (competed in 2)
- California Junior Open, San Francisco, CA, Grade 11
- U.S. High School National Championship, Grade 9: Division IV; Grade 10: Division III; Grade 11: Division II, placed 26th out of 85
- For a complete list of tournaments, see U.S. Squash Player Profile: www.mysquashprofile.com.

Camps

- Talbott Squash Academy, Stanford University, Grade 10
- Squash and Beyond Camp, Williams College, Grades 9–11
- Princeton Squash Camp, Princeton University, Grades 9–10
- Coach Contact Information:
  Mary Smith, High School · (201) 555-5555 · MSmith@gmail.com
  Bob Berk, Athletic Club · (201) 666-6666 · BBerk@TAC.edu

Academics

- 3.23 GPA
- SAT: 550 CR, 530 M, 600 W (January 2012)
- Planning to retake SATs in May 2012

Other Extracurricular Activities

- Varsity Tennis Team, Grades 9–11
- President of Key Club, Grade 11; Secretary of Key Club, Grade 10
- Board Member of Environmental Awareness Club, Grade 11
- Volunteer at Catholic Worker soup kitchen, Grades 9–11

Outside Interests

- Environmentally conscious living
- Grow over a dozen different fruits and vegetables in family garden; distribute what we don't eat to the Catholic Worker soup kitchen
  - Responsible for household composting
  - Collect compost from four neighbors
- Started campaign to recycle electronics at our local Y community center; have collected over thirty used electronic devices for proper recycling
- Yoga enthusiast
  - Practice Vinyasa yoga three times each week

7. WRITE A COVER LETTER

When you send copies of your resume, you'll want to attach a brief cover letter introducing yourself to the coach. Keep the letter short and sweet, remembering to show enthusiasm for the school by including one or two details about the college. Here's a sample:

> Dear Coach X,
>
> I am a junior at Sacred Heart High School in Delray Beach, Florida, who is interested in attending and playing golf for George Washington University. I will be playing first position on my varsity golf team this coming spring. My resume includes Junior Golf competition in the AJGA, Met PGA, IJGT, WMGA, and LIGA. When not on the golf course, I can often be found reading biographies, and I am especially interested in political science, which is one of the reasons that I would love to learn more about GW. I believe that the university is a good match for my academic interests and would also give me the opportunity to pursue my passion for golf.
>
> Please find my Athletic-Academic Profile enclosed as well as a DVD with some footage from my latest golf tournaments. I would love to speak with you more about your golf program and the recruiting process. I'll also keep you updated with regard to my Sacred Heart season and Junior Golf competitions.
>
> Thank you for your interest, I hope to hear from you soon.
>
> Very respectfully,
> Sarah Summit

Note how Sarah includes some information about her academic interests and shows how she would be a good match for George Washington in the classroom as well. She sounds warm and enthusiastic, but she keeps the letter short. Because this letter is an introduction, she lays the groundwork for additional contact with the coach by promising that she will keep the coach posted on her progress.

8. MAKE A VIDEO

The purpose of an athletic video isn't to show off your filmmaking abilities; it's to show coaches what you look like in action. So ask your parents or friends to get out their iPhones or video cameras at your games or matches and start filming. Then you can use the footage to put together a short segment of a game or a series of clips that showcase your abilities (this varies by sport, so it's a good idea to do some research about what coaches in your sport like to see). Don't worry too much about the video production aspect as long as a viewer can see your skills in a variety of situations. For example, if you play softball, you should probably have some shots of you fielding the ball as well as hitting. And don't forget to show it to your high school coach or a trusted, knowledgeable friend for feedback. People who have seen you play can help you evaluate whether the video clips capture your ability.

9. SEND OUT PACKETS

Now that you have your list of colleges, the coaches' contact information, as well as your resume, cover letter, and video, you are ready to start communicating with the people who will eventually decide if you are a good match for their teams. In addition to your resume, cover letter, and video, you should include a copy of your transcript in the packets because coaches can't recruit students who don't fit their college's academic profile. It is advisable to send these packets by the winter of junior year. This gives you enough time to communicate with coaches through the spring of junior year and the summer before senior year. Getting these packets out early is also an advantage if you're considering playing certain summer tournaments or attending sports camps where college coaches like to scout for recruits. They may remember your name and credentials from your packet before they meet you in person at one of these events.

10. FOLLOW UP

Some time after you send your packets to coaches, you may receive a response over email or the phone. If a coach writes to you, be sure to follow up with a polite response indicating your interest in learning more about the college team. This is also a good time to ask questions about certain camps or tournaments that you are considering attending over the summer and if the coach will also be there. Limit your questions to a couple of important ones because this is still early in the process and you want to make a good impression by respecting the fact that the coach is busy. If you don't hear from a coach within two weeks after you send your packets, you can write an email to inquire whether or not the coach has received the packet and restating that you're excited to find more about the school. Don't be discouraged if you don't hear right away. It may just be that the coach is busy.

STUDENTS OF COLOR AND FIRST-GENERATION COLLEGE STUDENTS

College admissions and race have been intertwined since affirmative action was first introduced in the 1960s in response to centuries of racial and gender discrimination in the United States. After the civil rights movement, historically white colleges wanted to do more to integrate their campuses and adopted a range of affirmative action policies to ensure that they would enroll a more diverse student body. The most controversial of these—racial quotas—was deemed unconstitutional by the Supreme Court in the famous Bakke case of 1978. In response, colleges adopted a policy called "holistic review," which is still in effect at most selective campuses today. A *holistic review* of applications means that admissions officers consider many different things beyond academics in their admissions decisions, including essays, recommendation letters, and interviews. Most college admissions officers will also consider whether or not a student can contribute to the diversity on campus, and that may give students from historically underrepresented groups a "plus" in the admissions process.

Unlike when it was first introduced, affirmative action is now seen as a way to enhance the diversity of college campuses and to improve the educational quality. Most college administrators believe that students learn better in heterogeneous groups that can expose them to new ideas and points of view, and students also tend to want more diverse learning environments, according to various studies that have been conducted over the years. Therefore, college admissions officers seek to recruit and admit students who are statistically underrepresented in their applicant pool. The vast majority of colleges will give a "plus" to African-American, Latino, and Native American students. However, some colleges give less of a "plus" to African students of Caribbean descent (as opposed to applicants with four American grandparents who are likely descended from slaves) and to upper- and middle-class Latino students. Although Asian-Americans are generally overrepresented in the selective college applicant pool, some rural, liberal arts colleges consider them in the "plus" category because Asian-Americans as a group tend to prefer more urban institutions with strong math and science programs. Asian-American students who are eager to boost their admissions chances should consider looking at some selective, small, rural, liberal arts colleges that want to increase the number of Asian-American students on campus.

In more recent years, students who are the first in their family to go to college have also been considered underrepresented on college campuses, and many admissions officers are extending a "plus" in the admissions process to this group, regardless of their race or ethnicity. On page 2 of the Common Application, there are questions about your parents' employment and education. Admissions officers look closely at where your parents went to college for two reasons. The first is that they want to see whether or not you are a legacy student, which I discuss in the next section of this chapter. The second is because they want to see if you are the first in your family to go to college. Admissions officers know that if your parents went to college, they are more likely to do the things that will help you prepare to go to college—things like encouraging reading, taking you to museums, sending you to after-school enrichment programs, and so on. If your parents did not go to college, you might not have been groomed for higher education in the same way. Because of this, many admissions officers want to make sure that first-generation college students get thoughtful consideration in the admissions process.

Just how big of a "plus" do students of color and first-generation college students receive in the admissions process? This is a very hard question to answer because it varies so much among colleges. In the past decade, states like California, Texas, and Florida have eliminated this kind of affirmative action for their public colleges. Most selective colleges still practice some form of these policies, but no one who is wholly unqualified gets into a certain college just because of their race or parental education. In my first book, *Fat Envelope Frenzy: Five Promising Students and the Pursuit of the Ivy League Prize*, I documented the journey of Marlene Fernandez, a talented low-income, Dominican-American student from New Rochelle, New York, who was the first in her family to go to college. Marlene was an A/B student in challenging courses with solid SAT scores who was turned down by all the reach schools on her list. Fortunately, she was accepted to several great colleges and graduated from Brandeis University in Massachusetts in 2011. However, the point remains: just because you belong to a group that benefits from affirmative action does not mean that you can go to any university you want.

When conducting your college search, students who are the first in their families to go to college and/or identify themselves as students of color should ask the same questions that all other B students must consider: Is this the right place for me? Can I get in?

The answer to the question about college fit is just as important, if not more so, than whether or not you can get into a particular college. Sometimes schools that try hardest to recruit students of color or first-generation college students do so because they don't have many on campus. You have to ask yourself these questions: Would I be happy being one of the only students from my background at this school? Would it be easier for me to succeed in college if I'm surrounded by people who are like me? Is it important for me to have access to faculty members who I can identify with because we have a shared background? Everyone has different answers to these questions. However, all students need to be honest with themselves about what makes them comfortable and happy before they commit to spending four years at a college that might not be able to offer them what they need.

As for the second question—can I get in?—first-generation college students and/or students of color need to meet the academic qualifications for admission just like any other applicant. Be sure to apply to a range of reaches, likelies, and safety schools.

LEGACIES

In most countries, universities determine their admissions policies based on students' performance in high school and/or on college entrance exams. We've already established that American colleges are unique in that they consider many different factors, but the most unusual might just be what is known as an applicant's "legacy" status. Most colleges will consider you a *legacy* if one of your parents graduated from the school, but some colleges will include grandchildren and siblings of graduates in this category as well. (You'll need to check with the colleges on your list for their particular policies.) If you happen to love the college that will consider you a legacy, you're in luck. Legacy applicants get a boost in the admissions process.

Colleges want to give special consideration to legacy students for two reasons. The first is to court alumni who fund endowments. This is done directly by admitting certain students and indirectly by publicizing the number of legacies who were admitted each year to the alumni body as a whole. The second reason that colleges love legacy students is that the yield on these students tends to be higher. These are people who grew up listening to Mom's stories about her favorite literature class or Dad's tales of his fraternity road trips, wearing college-branded sweatshirts, and rooting for their parents' alma maters in sports. Many of them have already formed an allegiance with the college and are more likely to accept an offer of admission than a student without this type of connection.

In addition to favoring legacy applicants in the admissions process, many colleges also have special services for legacy applicants, like special information sessions and campus tours. Some colleges will even allow you to schedule an appointment with an admissions officer in your junior year in high school to get tips and advice on boosting your chances of admission. If you are interested in attending a college that one or both of your parents went to, call the alumni relations department on campus and ask if the school offers these services to children of alumni.

How much of a boost do legacies get in the admissions process? The most useful statistic you can get your hands on is the legacy admission rate (that is, the percentage of legacy students who are accepted to this college), which is often twice as high as the regular admissions rate. Some colleges are happy to give you this statistic if you ask, while others are cagey about answering this question. If you do manage to get this information, remember to keep two things in mind: legacies tend to apply early (thus receiving the boost from early admissions that I described in chapter 6), and legacies have educated parents who are more likely to get them tutors and other types of support. Some of their higher rates of admission can be attributed to the leg up they have in life. It is important to understand that B students with Ivy League dreams will still have a hard time getting into these schools through the regular admissions process—even with legacy status. In general, less selective colleges are more likely to bend over backward for children of alumni because they are more concerned with fund-raising and want to boost their yields. Like all students, legacies need to do their homework about their chances of getting in.

TALENTED STUDENTS

Are you an outstanding tuba player who could make a splash in the marching band? Have your short stories been published? Did your film take second place in a student film festival? If so, you may also get a boost in the admissions process because of your talents. These talents go a long way toward making you the kind of interesting candidate that admissions officers remember. Colleges want students who will explore their passions—and eventually make a contribution to the campus community by sharing their talents.

If you are a student with a unique talent, be sure to include this information in your accomplishments doc (many colleges will also allow artists to submit portfolios of their work and musicians can send recordings of their music). It's also important to talk to your guidance counselor about putting some details about your talent in the guidance counselor recommendation. If you want to go a step further, consider contacting a college professor or staff member who might be interested in having you on campus. I worked with a talented tuba player who introduced himself to the marching band directors at each of his top five colleges. It wasn't hard! He just looked up their email addresses, wrote them a few lines about his experience, and said that he was eager to learn more about the marching band program. A few email exchanges later, two of these band directors offered to put in a good word with the admissions office and he ended up getting into his first-choice college. Talk about a high-yield investment!

If you love poetry, write to a poetry professor. If you want to DJ for a radio show, find the person who runs the campus station. If you dream of being the next Mother Teresa, contact the community service office. The good news is that you have nothing to lose by reaching out to people on campus who value your talents. Even if they don't offer to support you in the admissions process, they still might be able to give you an insider's perspective in an area that you care about and help you determine whether or not a particular school has the resources to help you take your talent or passion to the next level.

CHAPTER 9 ACTION STEPS

❏ If you are an athlete hoping to get recruited by a college coach, follow the ten steps outlined in this chapter.

❏ Most college admissions officers value diversity and seek to admit qualified students who are members of underrepresented minority groups, but these students should still think carefully about fit and consider how the colleges on their list will support them in reaching their full potential.

❏ Though many colleges give a "plus" to children of alumni, legacy applicants must still do their homework about the admissions process—there are no guarantees.

❏ If you are a student with a unique talent, detail it in your accomplishments doc, consider submitting a portfolio, encourage your guidance counselor to describe it in her letter of recommendation, and make contact with professors who might be interested in having you on campus.

CHAPTER 10

COMMUNICATING YOUR EXPERIENCE:

STUDENTS WITH LEARNING DISABILITIES

Here is a common scenario: Sam is a senior at a good suburban high school near San Francisco. When she was in middle school, she was diagnosed with *dyslexia*, a learning disability that makes it difficult for her to process what she reads. Over the years, she has learned how to cope by seeing a reading specialist twice a week and spending more time on her schoolwork than most of her friends. Her hard work has paid off in good grades—Bs, B+s, and the occasional A-. Standardized tests, however, are another story. Sam's highest ACT score was a 24 despite working with a tutor and taking prep classes for the better part of a year.

By the time senior fall rolls around, Sam has her list of colleges and is ready to begin work on her applications, but she is terrified that her ACT score is going to hold her back. Sam feels strongly that the test result is not representative of her ability and wonders if she should explain her learning disability to colleges and how she has worked to overcome it. Everyone she asks seems to give her a different answer. Some people say that colleges will just hold her disability against her and assume that she won't be able to do the work if they admit her. Others assure her that disclosing her disability will put the ACT score in context and encourage admissions officers to focus on her grades. These mixed messages drive Sam crazy. She wants to show colleges that she has much more to offer than her ACT scores might indicate, but she is concerned that she'll scare them away if she reveals her learning disability. What should she do—reveal her learning disability or not? This chapter gives the answers to this and other common questions for students with learning disabilities.

In the more than ten years that I have been helping students through the college application process, I've worked with many bright, talented high schoolers who had been diagnosed with learning disabilities. In fact, learning disabilities are so common that approximately one in seven Americans has some type of learning disability, according to the National Institutes of Health. Being diagnosed with a learning disability means that your brain works a little differently, but it certainly *does not* mean that you are stupid. Some of history's greatest thinkers had learning disabilities—Albert Einstein had serious problems with memory and reading, Leonardo da Vinci wrote backward because of dyslexia, and Thomas Edison was labeled as a "problem child" in school because of his poor organization and attention issues. Learning disabilities have nothing to do with intelligence.

As individuals, we each have unique strengths, weaknesses, passions, interests, and ways of communicating. Even though school curricula are often designed as one-size-fits-all, not everybody learns in the same way. Students with learning disabilities have particular difficulties receiving, processing, analyzing, and storing information that can impact their ability to read, write, spell, calculate, listen, reason, and understand. No one knows exactly how students develop these disabilities, but scientists suspect that they result from a combination of genetic and environmental factors. While the "disability" label may sound scary, the good news is that students who have been diagnosed with learning disabilities have more options for academic support than ever before. Your disability doesn't—and shouldn't—define who you are as a student or a person. With the right resources, and personal commitment on your part, you can achieve any academic goal you set your mind to.

COMMON TYPES OF LEARNING DISABILITIES

Students with learning disabilities usually exhibit a noticeable gap between their performance in the classroom and their potential for academic success. For example, someone with *dysgraphia*, a learning disability that impacts writing, may be able to express her thoughts verbally but will find it difficult to write them down in a way that other people understand. Other types of learning disabilities include dyslexia (a developmental reading disorder), *dyscalculia* (associated with difficulties in counting, estimating, measuring, and identifying patterns or organizing ideas), *auditory processing disorders* (difficulty taking in information through sound), *visual processing disorders* (difficulty taking in information through sight), and *attention deficit/hyperactivity disorder* (a disorder characterized by lack of attention, hyperactivity, and difficulty controlling impulses that can interfere with learning).

The first step in addressing a neurological problem that makes it harder for you to learn is to understand what causes it. The good news is that all public school students are entitled by law to a learning disability evaluation. During the evaluation process, you will put together a support team of teachers, psychologists, and other learning experts who will observe, interview, and test you to understand more about your problems in the classroom. When the evaluation is complete, you will receive a written report with your "diagnosis." This can either be a specific learning disability, like dyslexia or dyscalculia, or a general category of learning disabilities such as problems with audio or visual processing. (You can use this report later on if you need to apply for accommodations on standardized tests.)

Once you understand more about your learning disability, you can work with your evaluation team to design an Individualized Educational

Plan (IEP) to put the findings from your evaluation into practice. Your IEP is like your personal "user's manual" for learning. It describes the challenges you face and identifies ways to help you overcome them. For example, if you have an auditory processing disorder, you might be able to use a special note-taking machine in class so that you can see your teachers' lectures written down on a piece of paper instead of having to take in that information through listening alone. If you are dyslexic and read more slowly than other students, you'll probably get extra time on tests that involve reading comprehension. Your IEP will also give you a chance to write down your specific goals for the school year and a baseline so that you can measure your progress once you start using the support services that can help you learn better.

LEARNING DISABILITIES AND STANDARDIZED TESTING FOR COLLEGE

As if giving up your Saturday morning to take a grueling, four-hour, high-stakes standardized test wasn't bad enough, students with certain learning disabilities face additional challenges on the SAT and ACT. Fortunately, the College Board and ACT Inc. both allow students with learning disabilities to apply for testing accommodations—extra time, breaks during the test, a private room, the use of a computer, and so on. These accommodations create better test-taking conditions for students who have problems with reading, math, writing, attention, and/or processing. To be eligible for accommodations, you have to show both how your learning disability impacts your test taking *and* how the accommodations that you request will help you overcome this obstacle so that your test results will better reflect your true abilities.

Testing Accommodations

TESTING OBSTACLE	ACCOMMODATION
Taking in information by sight	• Large print • Fewer items on each page • An assigned reader to read you the questions or an audio recording of the questions • Colored paper • Use of a highlighter • Colored overlays • Braille
Responding to questions	• A scribe who can write the answers you verbally dictate • A computer (with or without a spell-checker) to type your essay responses • Large block answer sheet
Attention or scheduling issues	• Breaks during the test • Extra time • Extra days (you can break the test up into two days instead of one) • Adjustments to time of day • Small group setting • Private room • Screens to block out distractions
Facilities	• Lighting adjustments • Acoustic adjustments • Special furniture or tools • Alternative test site • Particular seating arrangement

If you have been diagnosed with a learning disability, be as proactive as possible about applying for accommodations that will give you the best chance of getting a good test score. There is no downside. Technically speaking, it is illegal for colleges to discriminate against students with learning disabilities in any way. However, paranoid students can rest assured because admissions officers have no way of knowing who received extra time or took the test in a private room. Many years ago, in response to lawsuits from disability rights activists, the testing agencies decided that they would no longer "flag" students who received accommodations.

Here is what you need to know about applying for standardized testing accommodations:

- **You need an official evaluation that documents your disability.** Testing agencies tend to prefer evaluations done by trained school staff over private psychologists, but both are acceptable. Just be sure that the relevant information is *clearly written* and not buried in hundreds of pages of paperwork. If you have a huge paper trail, ask your school psychologist to summarize the findings in a cover letter.

- **Your request has a better chance of being approved if you have a long history of documentation.** In recent years, the media has raised questions about whether students try to game the system and get a boost on standardized test scores by applying for accommodations that they don't really need. As a result, testing agencies have become more wary of students who get evaluated for learning disabilities right before the test. The College Board requires a learning disability diagnosis at least four months prior to the test (PSAT, SAT, SAT Subject Tests, AP exams), and the ACT wants documentation at least a year prior to the test. Students with a learning disability diagnosis in high school are going to be under more scrutiny than those who were diagnosed in elementary or middle school.

- **Testing agencies want to see that you use the accommodations you request on a regular basis in school.** Their logic goes like this: if you don't need extra time or a quiet room for test taking in school, you don't need it for the SAT. Informal arrangements with teachers don't count—you need to show documentation that you have been using specific testing accommodations in school for a significant period of time. If you are using support services in the classroom, ask your teachers to describe these services in writing.

- **If you want to apply for testing accommodations, make sure that you submit your paperwork early.** Although the vast majority of applicants eventually receive accommodations—the College Board approves 85 percent of accommodation requests and

ACT Inc. signs off on 92 percent (according to the *New York Times*)—it is not uncommon for the testing agencies to ask you for more paperwork or for them to turn you down the first time you submit a request. I suggest getting your application in *at least* six months in advance of your first test.

- **Some students need to appeal the decision two or three times before the agency finally gives in.** Because the testing agencies want to see a long history of documented learning disability accommodations, your chances of having to appeal a rejection are higher if you have been diagnosed as a teenager rather than earlier in life. Don't give up if you feel strongly that you need these accommodations to do well on these important tests. Most requests eventually get approved.

COMMUNICATING WITH ADMISSIONS OFFICERS ABOUT YOUR DISABILITY: DO'S AND DON'TS

Even though our society has come a long way in terms of awareness and understanding about learning disabilities, many students are afraid to talk about their disabilities in their college applications. The heart of their fear is simple: they are scared that admissions officers will think that they're not as smart as the other applicants or that they will have problems doing the work in college because of brain circuitry. In a perfect world, no student with a learning disability would ever feel ashamed or even shy about sharing this part of his life with others. Unfortunately, the college admissions process is a long way from being perfect.

The decision of whether or not to disclose a learning disability is completely up to you. Legally speaking, colleges are not allowed to ask you about it and they are not allowed to discriminate against you because of it. In general, you should opt to disclose your learning disability if you think it will help admissions officers put your academic record in context or understand more about what makes you tick.

Here are some situations where it is a good idea to include information about your learning disability in your application:

- You need to explain particularly low grades in certain subjects. Admissions officers are going to see that D in trigonometry or the C- in Spanish. Understanding more about your learning disability will help them put those isolated grades in context and reassure them that you are not lazy or apathetic.
- Your grades are much stronger than your standardized test scores. If you can explain how your learning disability made it difficult for you to do well on the SAT or ACT, admissions officers will be more likely to focus on your consistently strong high school record.
- You did not take certain high school courses that the college recommends or requires of high school applicants. It is important for colleges to know that your learning disability prevented you from taking certain classes, like an intensive foreign language or a more rigorous math course. Admissions officers may otherwise wrongly assume that you didn't want to challenge yourself, or they may disqualify you from admissions because you didn't take some of the courses that they generally recommend or require.
- You pulled your grades up after being diagnosed with a learning disability. If you did not have a formal evaluation until tenth or eleventh grade, then you may not have known how to cope with your learning disability for a large part of your academic career. Colleges will cut you some slack for the lower grades that you received early on if you were able to turn things around once you understood more about how to get support for your disability.
- Your learning disability has shaped you as a person and influenced your extracurricular activities and/or your future career path. Admissions officers want passionate and interesting students on their campuses. If you have become an advocate for learning disabilities or been impacted by your disability in other ways, feel free to share this part of yourself.

A great way to communicate with admissions officers about a learning disability is to include a letter to the admissions committee about your learning disability and how it has impacted your academic record in the "additional information" section of the Common Application. When writing this letter, don't apologize for your learning disability or wallow in self-pity. Instead, explain to the admissions committee what you have learned about yourself and how you have overcome the challenges you faced in the classroom. Address any particular weaknesses in your grades and test scores and explain why they are not representative of your abilities as a student. Show the admissions committee how smart and self-aware you are by writing in an insightful way. Describe how determined you are to do well in school and the steps you have taken to master the obstacles you have faced in the classroom. Do some research on the resources that the college has to support students with learning disabilities and write about how you plan to use them, if you are admitted to the school.

The following is an excerpt from a real letter written by a real student describing how his learning disability impacted his high school grades:

> Having spent several hours constructing and editing a very thorough essay on the twentieth-century transformation of Times Square for my tenth-grade history course, I was looking forward to seeing the results of my efforts in the form of a good grade. Mr. Smith arrived in high spirits and soon began to pass out the big pile of essays in his hands. As I turned the paper over I saw, to my disbelief, a big B written on the back. Good ideas, Tom. You're very astute, and such an articulate writer . . . but your organization is lacking here. Arrange things more clearly, make the reader's life easier.
>
> This situation is all too common in my life: points deducted from an otherwise quality essay because I find it difficult to organize my thoughts. I was recently tested for and learned that I had the profile of someone with nonverbal learning disability (NVLD). As it turns out, I have a large disparity of three standard deviations between my verbal and nonverbal subtests,

which led me to have a verbal IQ in the 99th percentile and a performance IQ in the 75th percentile. This means that I am very articulate in my speech and writing style, and that I have very high SAT scores, but I often have a difficult time functioning with an effective degree of organization, which is reflected in my grades. Having NVLD also makes it challenging for me to plan and keep track of things, which sometimes leads me to turn in assignments late, particularly assignments with multiple or long-term deadlines. Classes in areas such as science and mathematics are especially difficult if I am asked to manipulate and apply equations in more than a rote manner.

Though it took me until the eleventh grade to find out exactly why there was this disparity between my intellectual abilities and my grades, the diagnosis was nonetheless enlightening. I have made a commitment to improve some of my learning weaknesses by working with a cognitive behavioral therapist to cope with some of my processing challenges and to stay on top of my schedule and my organization. I am also communicating better with my teachers so that they understand the areas in which I need a little more help than other students.

As a result of these changes, my grades have been steadily improving, as has my confidence. I am optimistic that I will continue to progress as a student in college. Not only have I learned about my weaknesses in the classroom and how to cope with them, I have also learned more about the areas in which I excel. I can't wait to focus on the subjects that I love so that I can finally fulfill my potential.

This letter works because it is personal and honest. Tom helps admissions officers understand how he felt when the hard work he put into an assignment was not rewarded with a good grade without wallowing in self-pity or being self-depreciating. He uses clear language to explain his disability and isn't afraid to talk about his strengths as well as his weaknesses. Tom sounds like someone who has faced a setback and is committed to overcoming it. It also helps that he was able to pick up his grades after his diagnosis and get support when he needed it.

Here are some questions to help guide you in writing a letter to the admissions committee about your learning disability:

- When did you first learn that you had a learning disability?
- What challenges do you face as a consequence of your learning disability?
- How have you addressed these challenges? What support services or techniques have you used?
- What academic accomplishments are you most proud of? (Be specific.)
- What steps have you taken to learn about learning disability support services in college?
- What specific learning disability support services do you plan to use in college?
- How have you grown as a student during your time in high school?
- How do you hope to grow as a student in college?

Once you have written this letter, you may also want to share it with your guidance counselor. Your guidance counselor is charged with giving colleges a "big picture" assessment of your academic performance, so it makes sense that she may want to discuss your learning disability and how you cope with it in the recommendation letter. Because you want to focus on the positive aspects of your academic record, I recommend having frank conversations with your counselor about the support strategies you have used to overcome your learning disability while stressing the bright spots in your academic record that highlight your potential for future success.

FINDING COLLEGES WITH GREAT SUPPORT SERVICES FOR STUDENTS WITH LEARNING DISABILITIES

As a student with a learning disability, you need to consider how you will cope with your disability in college. Your IEP will end after high school graduation and—just like in the "real world"—you won't be required to have a clear plan for learning in college. The responsibility for your performance rests with you. It is your job to set yourself up for success by choosing a college that can offer you the support you need to do your best in your classes.

Earlier in this book, I talked about how to come up with a list of priorities when choosing the colleges to which you will apply. The importance you place on finding a school with excellent learning disability support services should depend on the severity of your learning disability and the impact it has on your academic performance. The *K&W Guide to College for Students with Learning Disabilities* by Marybeth Kravetz and Imy Wax is a good place to start for some basic information about learning disability support services at three hundred different colleges. If your budget allows, you might also want to consider hiring an independent college counselor with experience in placing similar students in colleges that meet their needs. The Independent Education Consultant Association (IECA) has a searchable database on their website. Be sure to ask for references from past clients with learning disabilities.

Most colleges will have some type of academic support facilities, but you'll have to dig deeper to really understand how the college works with students. Ideally, you should schedule an appointment to speak with an administrator who specializes in learning disability support when you visit the campus. If you can't make it there in person, reach out to someone by phone or email. Here are some questions to ask about learning disability support and accommodations:

- Can students with learning disabilities petition the registrar to waive certain graduation requirements? (Example: If you have an auditory processing disorder that makes it difficult to learn foreign languages, can you petition to get out of the foreign language requirement?)

- Do professors offer testing accommodations to students who need it? What is the process for requesting accommodations? Have there been any complaints about faculty who are resistant to accommodating students with learning disabilities?
- Will I have access to a learning disability coach or case manager? Or will I have to manage my own support services and accommodations?
- Do students with learning disabilities have a special orientation program to help them transition?
- How many full-time staff members work with students who need learning disability support? Do they have any special training for this work?
- Is tutoring available for all classes? Is there a cost? When are the tutors available? Is there a waiting list for tutoring services? How are the tutors selected and trained?
- Are there any courses on study skills, writing skills, and/or time management?
- Can students with learning disabilities petition to take a lighter load of courses?
- Do you have any data on the graduation rates of students with learning disabilities? How does this differ from the overall graduation rates?

ADDITIONAL RESOURCES FOR STUDENTS WITH LEARNING DISABILITIES

Here are some organizations that you might want to check out for additional information about applying to college with a learning disability:

- Learning Disabilities Association of America (www.ldanatl.org)
- National Center for Learning Disabilities (www.ncld.org)

- LD Online (www.ldonline.org)
- Attention Deficit Disorder Association (www.add.org)
- International Dyslexia Association (www.interdys.org)
- National Institute of Neurological Disorders and Stroke (www.ninds.nih.gov)

CHAPTER 10 ACTION STEPS

❏ If you suspect you have a learning disability, get a formal evaluation and use the results to create an Individualized Education Plan, which is like a personal "user's manual" for your learning needs.

❏ If you have been diagnosed with a learning disability, be proactive about applying for any accommodations that will give you the best chance of getting a good test score.

❏ You should disclose your learning disability in your college application if you find yourself in one of these situations:
  - You have low grades in certain subjects.
  - Your grades are much stronger than your test scores.
  - You were unable to take certain recommended high school courses because of your disability.
  - Your grades improved after your diagnosis.
  - Your learning disability has shaped you as a person and influenced your extracurricular activities and/or future career path.

❏ Use the guiding questions in this chapter to help you write a letter or essay about your disability to the admissions office, if you decide to disclose this information.

CHAPTER 11

PAYING FOR COLLEGE

Just because you *want* a BMW convertible and the BMW sales rep *wants* to sell it to you doesn't mean that you'll be driving to school tomorrow with the top down. Even though the bulk of this book is dedicated to helping motivated students like you find and get into your dream college, it is just as important that you figure out how to pay the tuition bill once you're accepted. Unfortunately, there's a little thing called money that often gets in the way between what we want and what we can have. Though it might not seem fair to hard-working students holding college acceptance letters, the rules of commerce apply to college—you've got to pay the bill to get the diploma.

You'll probably want to sit down the first time you look at the cost of tuition, room, board, and fees at a typical American college. The full cost of one year at an American private college—what we call the "sticker price"—can easily reach $35,000 and can even climb to

$55,000 for the most expensive schools. Sticker prices at in-state public colleges are not quite as insane but still high—around $25,000 for one year of tuition, room, board, and fees. If you're like most teenagers in the country, there's no way that your parents can write these huge checks to your Dream U. The good news is that it is possible to pay for college without selling a vital organ or mortgaging your parents' house. For students in need, the two most important words in the English language might just be "financial aid."

Like nuclear physics or the NCAA tournament, financial aid awards are complicated. Although the sticker price to attend Trinity College in Hartford, Connecticut, is about $46,000, you could walk into a Trinity dorm and find that everyone living on the second floor is paying a different amount. Some students will finance college with *grants* and *scholarships* (money that does not have to be paid back), some students have loans that they will have to repay after graduation, some students' parents borrowed money to pay the bills, while other students will work to contribute to their college costs. Most students will finance college through a combination of these methods.

Because of all the variables involved, it is important to be informed about financial aid. This chapter will give you crucial tips, a comprehensive glossary of terms, a full explanation of the application process, and everything you need to know about interpreting your financial aid awards so that you can eventually enroll in a school that you love—and can afford.

START WITH A BUDGET

As you'll see once we get into the nitty-gritty of the financial aid application process, the federal government and individual colleges tell you how much they expect you to contribute to college based on an analysis of your household finances. Depending on how they do their calculations, one school may report that you can afford $15,000 a year, while another may conclude that you can only contribute $10,000. None of this matters if your parents are paying for your grandmother's nursing home care and tell you that they can only contribute $5,000 toward college each year. This is why it is so important to come up with a realistic budget before you apply for aid instead of getting confused by different colleges telling you that you can afford different amounts.

Your budget should consist of two important numbers: your out-of-pocket contribution and your debt limit. The *out-of-pocket* number is what you and your parents can pay directly to the college from your family's income and savings. Your *debt limit* is the total amount of debt you feel comfortable taking on to finance your undergraduate education. Believe it or not, the vast majority of financial aid awards contain money that you will have to repay in the years after college. So why are loans considered "financial aid?" Because these loans are either *subsidized* (meaning that the government will pay your interest until six months after graduation) or have favorable terms like fixed interest rates and payment plans that keep in mind that you won't be able to pay while you're still toiling away in class.

Figure out how much debt you are willing to take on *before* you apply for financial aid—otherwise, you might find yourself taking on more than is feasible. Do you plan to go on to graduate school? Are you hoping to use your college degree to work at or start a nonprofit organization that will reward you in ways other than material wealth? Do your postgraduation plans include the words "struggling" and "artist"? If you answered yes to any of these questions, you're probably not a good candidate for excessive undergraduate debt and you should look at colleges that won't require you to take out big loans. It's also important to understand the different types of loans, as we'll discuss later in this chapter, so that you can make informed decisions about financing college that won't prohibit you from going after your dreams.

DON'T GET STICKER SHOCK

Believe it or not, a private college with a sticker price of $40,000 per year may actually be cheaper than a public college with a sticker price of $20,000. How is that possible? Some private colleges follow the model of high tuition–high aid, meaning that the students who can afford to do so pay an arm and a leg, while the college puts more money toward generous grants that bring down the cost of attendance for needy students. On the other hand, some in-state school systems work hard to keep their tuition and fees down for all students, meaning they don't have as much money left over for financial aid for individual students who need assistance. These states are supplementing the cost of college for *all* students, not just those who need financial aid.

The bottom line is, don't be scared off by the sticker price at your dream college. In-state public universities are great options for many students, but if your heart lies at a private college with an outrageous full-cost price tag, financial aid can help you close the price gap between your private and public college options. Believe it or not, your Dream U. might end up costing you less than the school you're about to settle for. You'll need to research all your options before you can compare costs.

ADD MORE SAFETY SCHOOLS TO YOUR LIST IF YOU NEED FINANCIAL AID

When the topic of financial aid comes up, one of the first questions that parents and students want an answer to is this: will applying for aid hurt my chances of getting into this school? The answer, as with most things relating to financial aid, is an unsatisfying *it depends*.

Colleges that are *need blind* do not take a family's financial circumstances into account when making admissions decisions; the same student has an equal chance of admission if he has a huge trust fund or if he needs a ton of financial aid. On the other hand, schools that are *need aware* do look at whether or not a student can pay the full sticker price when deciding whether or not to accept him: that means a borderline application might be put in the "admit" pile if the student isn't asking for any money from the college.

Just to confuse things further, many colleges don't advertise their need-blind/need-aware admissions policies, so you may have to do a little detective work to decipher the different policies for the colleges on your list. A good rule of thumb is that need-blind colleges tend to brag about the fact that they don't consider students' finances in admissions decisions, just like a wealthy "real housewife" might say that she goes shopping without looking at price tags. If a college uses vague language like "We meet 100 percent of need for *admitted* students" and doesn't come right out and say "Our admissions process is need blind," then they are probably not.

It would be a better and fairer world if all colleges were need blind, but, unfortunately, most schools just can't afford to make all their admissions decisions without calculating their financial aid budgets at the same time. Even more unfortunate is the fact that need-blind schools tend to be the wealthier, more selective colleges, which—let's face it—will be harder for students who are not at the top of their class to get into. Most colleges that cater to students like you are need aware.

Do not despair—you will find a great school that you can afford. There are two things you need to remember. The first is to add more safety schools to your list—two or three additional colleges—just to be cautious because, all things being equal, it might be slightly harder for you to get into a need-aware college if you ask for financial aid. The second thing you can do is to put together the best possible application by following the advice in this book. Most need-aware colleges only factor in a student's ability to pay for borderline cases, which means that if there are two students that the admissions committee likes but doesn't necessarily love, the one who can pay will have a better shot. Your job is to make the admissions committee love you so much that they won't care about the fact that saying yes to you costs just a little more money.

YOU WON'T KNOW WHAT YOU'LL GET UNTIL YOU APPLY

One of the things that makes it so hard to plan for college financially is that you won't know exactly how much, or what kind of, financial aid you'll get from a particular school until you apply. I encountered a very powerful example of how two different colleges can end up awarding the same student dramatically different financial aid packages when writing my first book, *Fat Envelope Frenzy*, in which I followed five ambitious students throughout their senior year of high school. Spoiler alert: One student, an Ethiopian-American math enthusiast named

Nabil, dreamed of going to MIT and was thrilled when he received an acceptance from this incredibly selective school. Unfortunately, his excitement deflated like helium from a leaky balloon when he read his financial aid award letter. Because his father owned the gas station at which he worked, MIT considered the value of the property as an asset. They expected his parents to borrow against the property or take out hundreds of thousands in student loans. But Nabil also got into Princeton—home to another one of the best math programs in the country. Princeton did not take the value of Nabil's father's gas station into account and awarded him generous grants based only on his family's income. Needless to say, Nabil didn't have to think too long about which college to attend. Four years later, he graduated from Princeton—debt free.

As Nabil's story shows, every college has its own system for calculating financial need. Things like retirement accounts, investments, house value, credit card debt, and medical expenses can be interpreted differently by schools. Even if two colleges agree on the amount they think your family can pay, they may give you wildly different options for making up the remainder of your college costs. Grants that you don't have to pay back are preferable to writing monthly checks to a student loan lender for ten or twenty years. Government loans are preferable to private loans, which carry higher interest rates and less flexible payback terms. The only way you can know the amount and type of financial aid that you will receive is to apply for financial aid from *each* college on your list. Then compare the offers.

THINK OF COLLEGE AS A FOUR-YEAR INVESTMENT

It takes four (and sometimes five or six) years to get a bachelor's degree. So you need to think of college as a four-year investment. For need-based financial aid, you will need to file your financial aid forms every year. Know that your award may change if your parents' financial situation changes. With merit-based aid, some scholarships are nonrenewable, which means that you'll only get this money for your first year, and then you're on your own. Sometimes scholarships have other strings attached, like GPA or work requirements. Because financial aid is awarded on an annual basis, it's a common mistake to budget only for the upcoming year. Thinking of college as a four-year enterprise means having all the information you need about how financial aid awards can potentially change over time.

The best way to get this information is to make friends with your financial aid officer. Most financial aid offices will divide up an incoming class, usually by last name, and assign particular administrators to work with individual students. The good news about this arrangement is that you'll have a designated point person to talk to, an expert who can walk you through the complex maze of financial aid. Take advantage of this resource by picking up the phone when you have questions. Financial aid officers are generally friendly people who are interested in helping students figure out how to afford college costs. Here are some important questions to ask:

- Is my grant and/or scholarship renewable?
- What are the conditions for the renewal of my grant and/or scholarship?
- Is there any way to get the grant and/or scholarship back if I lose it because my grades dip one semester?
- Does the grant and/or scholarship increase with tuition, or is it a fixed amount?
- What happens if I max out the limit on my government loan?
- If I get an outside scholarship, will the college reduce my financial aid?
- Because I have a younger sibling who is going to be in college in a few years, will you be able to make adjustments to my financial aid package? How do you calculate aid for families with multiple students in college?
- What will happen to my financial aid package if one of my parents loses a job or falls ill?
- Work-study is part of my financial aid package. (For more details on work-study, see "The Anatomy of a Financial Aid Award Letter" on page 176.) How do I get a work-study job?

How much do employers usually pay? What happens if I can't find one that fits with my schedule?

- I'm planning on double-majoring and still want to graduate on time. Can I get financial aid for summer course work if I need to take classes in the summer?
- I really want to study abroad one semester. What is the process for getting financial aid?
- How much has this college raised tuition and fees in the past? How do you suggest that I factor in expected increases in tuition and fees?

Trust me, you don't want to end up holding the bill for thousands of dollars because you didn't realize that your scholarship wasn't renewable, or find yourself in a position where you need to take out unexpected, inflexible private loans because you exceeded your government loan limit. Remember, college is a multiple-year commitment, so plan for the long term financially.

HOW DO YOU ACTUALLY GET FINANCIAL AID?

There are two major "types" of financial aid—need-based aid and merit-based aid. *Need-based aid* is awarded solely on the basis of your family's financial need for college, without regard to what kind of grades you have or whether or not you have a flawless half-court shot on the basketball court. *Merit-based aid* is awarded to applicants that the college wants to recruit—these can be B students with awesome SAT scores or unique talents in art, music, or athletics. Colleges often award merit-based aid without regard to whether or not students can pay tuition on their own. Therefore, wealthy students can get merit-based aid but not need-based aid; not-so-wealthy students are eligible for both types.

Though some B students will be eligible for merit-based aid, most financial aid for college is awarded on the basis of *financial need*, which is defined as the difference between what the college costs and what your family can afford to pay.

If you think you might qualify for need-based aid, you will have to apply. Here are some of the standard financial aid forms that you may be asked to complete to apply for need-based financial aid: Free Application for Federal Student Aid (FAFSA), College Scholarship Service Profile (CSS Profile), and state and institutional college forms. Let's take a closer look at each of these forms.

FREE APPLICATION FOR FEDERAL STUDENT AID (FAFSA)

The FAFSA is the most popular type of financial aid application form because it is required for all aid from the federal government. (*Note:* Only U.S. citizens and permanent residents are eligible for federal financial aid.) You can fill out the FAFSA online at www.fafsa.ed.gov between January 1 and June 30 of your senior year of high school. After you and your parents complete all the questions about your family's income and assets, you will then get a Student Aid Report (SAR), which includes an estimate of your Expected Family Contribution (EFC) for college. This is the amount that the federal government estimates that you can pay for your college costs. Because the federal government does not consider certain assets like the value of your home or your parents' retirement accounts, the EFC you'll get from your FAFSA may be lower than the EFC that will be calculated by a particular college. The lower your EFC, the higher your eligibility for federal financial aid, and vice versa. You can get an estimate of your federal EFC at any point before you fill out your FAFSA by using an online tool called the FAFSA4Caster (http://FAFSA4caster.ed.gov).

COLLEGE SCHOLARSHIP SERVICE PROFILE (CSS PROFILE)

Many private colleges, some public colleges, and several private scholarships will ask you to complete a CSS Profile (in addition to the FAFSA), which is available as early as October 1 of your senior year through the College Board (https://profileonline.collegeboard.com). Unlike the FAFSA, which is free, you'll have to pay a fee for each school to which you submit a CSS Profile. If you apply under an early admissions program with a deadline sometime in the fall of your senior year, the college's financial aid office will often use the CSS Profile to estimate your financial aid awards since the FAFSA is not available until January 1. The CSS Profile is even more in-depth than the FAFSA and may ask you questions about the value of your parents' home, how much money your parents have saved for your siblings' education, and whether or not your family has any ongoing medical expenses. If your parents are divorced and one or both of them has remarried, the CSS Profile will also ask you questions about your stepparents' finances. After you complete the CSS Profile, you might find that your EFC is different—sometimes higher, but not always—than the EFC you received on your Student Aid Report after completing the FAFSA. The CSS is available on October 1 so students can complete this form before the early decision/action deadlines.

STATE AND INSTITUTIONAL COLLEGE FORMS

In addition to or in lieu of the CSS Profile, you might be asked to fill out financial aid forms for individual colleges or for public colleges in certain states. Institutional forms may ask similar questions to those included in the CSS Profile about your family's assets (the value of your parents' house, retirement accounts, or any savings they have for your siblings) and their expenses (medical bills, private school or college tuition for your siblings, credit card debt, and so on). All of this information is designed to give financial aid officers more details about your household finances so that they can determine the amount and type of financial aid to offer you.

COMPLETING NEED-BASED FINANCIAL AID FORMS

It's spreadsheet time again! You'll need to keep track of the forms and deadlines that each college requires for the financial aid application process. Here's a sample that can work for you:

Sample: Financial Aid Application Forms and Deadlines

	COLLEGE 1	COLLEGE 2	COLLEGE 3
FAFSA deadline	Feb. 1		
CSS Profile deadline	• Nov. 1 for early decision • Feb. 1 for regular decision		
Deadline for other forms	N/A		
Documents required	• 2010, 2011 tax returns • Bank statements • IRA • 529 Plans		
Documents Sent	• FAFSA (Jan. 3) • CSS Profile (Nov. 15) • 2010, 2011 tax returns (Mar. 15) • Bank statements (Nov. 15) • IRA (Nov. 15) • 529 Plan (Nov. 15)		

Because different colleges have unique paperwork requirements, it's really important to stay organized. Using a spreadsheet will help ensure that you get all the correct paperwork in on time and have the best chance of getting a generous financial aid package. Here are some other tips to keep in mind as you apply for financial aid:

• **Make sure you have at least one parent with you when you fill out financial aid forms—unless you absolutely have to do it yourself—since most of the questions are about parental finances.** It's also perfectly fine to ask your parents to complete the forms on their own or ask an expert like a financial adviser or accountant, if they have one, to complete the forms.

• **Complete all financial aid forms as early as possible.** Financial aid funds are precious and limited. Your financial aid officer will have fewer options to work with if you apply late. For schools that require the CSS Profile, complete this form first and follow up with the FAFSA. Use estimates of your household income if your parents haven't filed your household taxes yet. You can submit the tax forms later on when they are ready.

• **Gather all your family's bank statements and tax records in one place *before* you sit down to complete financial aid forms.** The only thing more annoying than having to answer all these questions is getting up every five minutes to search for the documents that you need. If you get organized before you start filling out the forms, the process will go more smoothly.

- **Carefully review your Student Aid Report and report any errors immediately.** Anyone can make a mistake, especially when you're dealing with so many documents and questions. Be sure to address any errors as soon as you notice them—otherwise you could end up holding up the financial aid process and put yourself at a disadvantage for applying late.

THE ANATOMY OF A FINANCIAL AID AWARD LETTER

Once you complete all your paperwork (and if you are lucky enough to get accepted), you will receive your financial aid award letter. Here are some of the things that financial aid officers may consider when creating these letters:

- Cost of attendance (this should include tuition, fees, room, board, books, supplies, transportation, health insurance, and personal expenses)
- Family income
- Family size
- Number of family members in private school or college
- Parental savings
- Student savings
- Household debt
- Medical expenses
- Expenses associated with caring for a grandparent or other family members
- The value of your parents' house
- The value of investment or vacation properties
- The value of a family business
- Your parents' retirement accounts

- The value of your parents' life insurance policies
- How much your parents have saved for your siblings to go to college
- Scholarships or grants that you have received from other sources
- Academic accomplishments (some colleges may be more generous toward B students with high SAT scores than B students with low SAT scores because they are trying to increase their average standardized test scores)
- Athletic abilities

If you're lucky, your financial aid award will contain at least some money that is awarded in the form of a grant or scholarship that does not have to be repaid. In addition to merit-based scholarships, you may also be eligible for need-based grants from federal or state governments as well as from particular colleges on the basis of your household finances. The most common type of federal need-based grant is the *Pell Grant*, which was worth up to $5,500 in 2012–13. These grants are reserved for students with household incomes below $40,000, and the neediest Pell Grant recipients are also eligible for *Federal Supplemental Educational Opportunity Grants (FSEOG)*, which can go as high as $4,000. You can find out more about the different types of need-based federal grants, and up-to-date amounts, on the student aid website run by the U.S. Department of Education (http://studentaid.ed.gov). Some states also award need-based grants for college. Contact your state higher education agency to find out more about their need-based grants (www.sheeo.org/agencies.asp).

Your financial aid award letter may contain a *self-help component*, which includes *federal work-study jobs* and *loans*. Most financial aid awards ask students to contribute a small amount to their education through a work-study job. You might be thinking, *Why is this "financial aid" if the college is asking me to work?* Work-study jobs aren't like regular jobs that you might get off-campus; they're much more flexible and allow you to stay connected to your life at school. You might get to "work" at the library, which may give you some built-in study time, or do something that you can eventually put on your resume like plan events or lectures through the Student Affairs Office. Most importantly, work-study jobs operate on a student-friendly schedule, so you'll have time off to study for exams and go home to visit your parents during college holidays. Plus, they usually pay pretty well because the funding is supplemented by the federal government (another reason that they are considered "financial aid"), and there is a limit to how many hours you'll be allowed to work.

Though paying for college can be stressful, it is important to be realistic about the number of hours you can work while you are a full-time student. Over their college years, I see students make a lot of mistakes, but one of the biggest is working too many hours outside of school. I remember a particular young woman, we'll call her Brenda, who worked full-time at a local pharmacy while she was enrolled as a full-time college student—and *failed* half her first-semester classes as a result. Ironically, she also received much less financial aid in her second year of school because her university made her put almost all the money she earned toward paying for her college costs. It was a vicious cycle: Brenda worked to get money for school, she had no time for school, she failed her classes, which meant that she had to retake them and spend more money to graduate—not to mention the fact that she received decreased financial aid because of her job! Bottom line: Don't fall for the short-term rewards of demanding off-campus jobs. Instead, get your pocket money from student-friendly work-study jobs that have reasonable hours and keep you where you need to be—on campus.

Most students who qualify for financial aid will be offered *direct loans* from the federal government as part of their financial aid package for college. Even though they must be repaid with interest, direct loans from the federal government are considered "financial aid" because they almost always have lower fixed interest rates than private loans and more borrower-friendly terms. Here are some of the advantages of these loans:

- Direct loans give you flexible payback terms. You can choose how long you want to take to pay back the government. (You can, however, pay it back early if you strike it rich or win the lottery.) You can also choose a payment plan where your monthly payments start low and get higher over time, if you expect to be making more money as you get further into your career.

- Direct loans offer an *income-contingent repayment plan*, which means that your monthly payments will not go over a certain amount if you do not earn a lot of money. As long as you make payments equivalent to 20 percent of your discretionary monthly income for twenty-five years, your loan will be forgiven—even if you do not end up paying the full amount that you owe to the federal government. This repayment option is terrific for students who are considering entering low-paying but personally rewarding jobs in the nonprofit world or the arts.

- If you lose your job, have a serious illness, or face another economic hardship, you can apply for *deferment* or *forbearance*, which allow you to temporarily stop or adjust your direct loan payments without any penalties until you get back on your feet. You'll still have to pay back the money you owe the government, but you can negotiate the payback terms in an emergency—just be sure that you communicate with your lender about your circumstances in advance.

- If really bad things happen—you become permanently disabled, declare bankruptcy, or, God forbid, pass away—your family will not be responsible for your federal student loans. This is not the case, however, with nongovernment, private loans. Sounds crazy, but you read that correctly: you may have to repay your private loans if you declare bankruptcy and your estate may have to pay back the bank for your private student loans even if you die!

- Direct loans can also be forgiven if you work in certain public sector jobs, such as teaching at a low-income school for at least five years. This is called *loan forgiveness*. You can find out more about loan forgiveness on the U.S. Department of Education's Direct Lending website (http://studentaid.ed.gov).

There are two types of direct loans from the federal government: subsidized and unsubsidized. *Subsidized loans* are considered need-based financial aid because they are awarded to students based on household finances. If you qualify for a subsidized loan, the government will pay your interest and loan charges during the time that you are enrolled (at least half-time) as a student. *Unsubsidized loans* are not considered need-based financial aid because they are available to all students regardless of their family income, and students are responsible for the interest they accrue while they are enrolled in college. If they have decent credit, your parents will also be eligible for a *Direct PLUS Loan,* which carries a slightly higher interest rate than the federal loans available to students, but they are a good option for parents who can't afford to pay for college costs all at once.

There are limits on how much you as a student can borrow from the federal government. In 2011–12, dependent students (basically all high school seniors who live with their parents) could borrow a maximum of $31,000 with no more than $23,000 in subsidized loans for college. Because of this, some students also turn to *private loans* (loans from banks as opposed to the government) to make up the difference in college costs. Before you even think about taking out a private loan, make sure that you have maxed out the limits of your government loans. Here are some reasons that private loans are less favorable for students than direct loans from the federal government:

- They usually carry higher interest rates.
- Interest rates often fluctuate with the loan market, which means that you might get slightly different loan bills each month. This makes it hard to budget and plan over time.
- You will likely not have control over how long it takes you to pay these loans back and you will not be able to pay them back early, even if you want to.
- Most importantly, there are almost no circumstances under which you can get rid of these loans—even if you lose your job, get sick, are permanently disabled, declare bankruptcy, or die. That's why Elizabeth Warren, a U.S. senator from Massachusetts who specializes in bankruptcy, told the *Wall Street Journal* that private student lenders "have powers that would make a mobster envious."

Because private loans are so profitable, banks use all kinds of tricks to attract students, including giving them misleading information about federal loan requirements. Private lenders can also entice colleges to refer students to certain private student loan companies as "preferred lenders" on financial aid websites and award letters, even though they may not offer students favorable lending terms. Don't fall for these tricks! If you really can't get around taking out a private student loan, there are two things you need to do: (1) be sure that you only borrow the bare minimum amount; and (2) do your own research on the different loan companies instead of just going with your college's "preferred lender." The excellent website www.finaid.org has a private student loan comparison chart that is very helpful.

SHOW ME THE MONEY: OUTSIDE SCHOLARSHIPS

In addition to the financial aid that you might get from a college, there are literally hundreds of other college scholarships out there for B students. Lots of students falsely believe that the only way to get a scholarship is to have a perfect GPA, but plenty of scholarships are awarded on the basis of things like extracurricular interests or by organizations like Rotary clubs or places of worship that want to support local high school students. Many of these might be on the small side—say, $500 to $2,000—compared with the high cost of college, but they certainly add up (plus imagine how much it will impress your future employers to put a list of scholarships that you won on your resume). Think of your scholarship search like a game with two rules:

1. If you don't play, you can't win.
2. The more you play, the better your chances of hitting the jackpot.

Believe it or not, thousands of dollars in scholarship money goes unclaimed every year because of lack of applicants. So do your research and get in the game. Here's a list of some great websites that allow you to search for scholarships that you might qualify for. Once you know your options, cast a wide net by applying for numerous scholarships to increase your odds of winning money for college.

- www.collegescholarships.org
- www.collegetoolkit.com
- www.fastweb.com/college-scholarships
- www.finaid.org/scholarships
- www.petersons.com/college-search/scholarship-search.aspx
- www.scholarshipexperts.com
- www.scholarships.com
- www.nationalmerit.org
- www.meritaid.com

TIPS FOR APPLYING FOR OUTSIDE SCHOLARSHIPS

With thousands of outside scholarships available to high school students, it is easy to become overwhelmed, and it can be difficult to efficiently manage the application process. Here are some things to keep in mind when considering outside scholarships:

- **Make sure you qualify.** Don't waste your time applying for a scholarship if the GPA cutoff is a 3.7 and you have a 3.0 or if the award is for Hispanic students and you are Native American. Make a list of all your unique attributes—Are you editor of your high school newspaper? Are you active in your church? Have you done a lot of volunteer work in the community?—and look for scholarships that match. You can also search for scholarships by attributes like hometown, religion, race/ethnicity, and gender.
- **Keep track of deadlines.** The best way to make sure that you *won't* get a scholarship is to miss the deadline. Scholarship money is precious and deadlines are strict, so be sure to keep track of when the applications are due.
- **Follow the rules in this book for good essay writing.** Many scholarship applications will ask you to write an essay. Sometimes

you can use essays that you've already written for your college applications, but other times the questions are so specific that you'll need to write something new. The more work you put into your scholarship application essays, the better your chance at winning. If you follow the rules in this book for good essay writing, you'll be ten steps ahead of your competition.

- **Have someone you trust help you proofread your application.** When you get a rejection letter from a scholarship organization it never says, "We liked your application, but there were too many typos." However, the reality is that accuracy matters, and students lose out all the time because they didn't take five minutes to proofread their applications. Don't let a misspelled word or grammatical mistake come between you and hundreds of dollars.
- **Watch out for scams.** Sadly, there are plenty of scam artists out there looking to take advantage of vulnerable students. Here are two rules for spotting scholarship scams:

  1. Never pay for a scholarship application.
  2. Don't apply to any organization that "guarantees" you'll win money.

Remember, scholarships are competitive because there is not enough money to go around to every student with a college tuition bill. If a scholarship organization violates these basic principles, it's probably a scam.

CREATE A FINANCIAL AID WORKSHEET

Once you have your financial aid offers in hand, you'll need a convenient way to compare the different components. I recommend making a financial aid worksheet. This will help you calculate your true out-of-pocket costs and debt totals for each college.

Start by calculating the *total cost of attendance* for each school. Include not only the obvious expenses like tuition, fees, and room and board but also the cost of books, travel, lab fees, and entertainment. Think long and hard about what you might need to attend each college on your list. If the school is far from home, think about travel costs. If you're going to school in a big city, know that your expenses will be higher than in a college town. If you're moving to Vermont from Florida, you'll need to invest in good winter gear. Most colleges will not include these considerations in their cost of attendance estimates, so you will have to do some calculations on your own.

Once you know the total cost of attendance for each college on your list, you can deduct any grants that you receive. This calculation will bring you to an important number that represents the "self-help" portion of your aid award, or the amount that you and your parents are expected to contribute to your college costs. *Self-help* has three different components: loans, savings, and work-study. Your spreadsheet should have entries for each of these categories and should look something like the example shown on the opposite page.

Your spreadsheet will give you a better sense of your out-of-pocket expenses and your debt load at each of the colleges on your list for the first year of enrollment. Once you understand what you will be expected to contribute to attend the colleges on your list, you can compare these numbers with the budget you created at the beginning of the process.

Comparison of College Costs

		COLLEGE 1	COLLEGE 2	COLLEGE 3
1	Tuition			
2	Fees			
3	Room			
4	Board (including meal plans)			
5	Travel			
6	Health insurance (if not included in fees)			
7	Other (books, lab fees, new clothes)			
8	**TOTAL COST OF ATTENDANCE (ADD LINES 1 THROUGH 7)**			
9	Scholarships/grants			
10	Work-study			
11	**TOTAL NONDEBT FINANCIAL AID (ADD LINES 9 AND 10)**			
12	Federal subsidized loans (student)			
13	Federal unsubsidized loans (student)			
14	Federal unsubsidized loans (parent)			
15	**TOTAL GOVERNMENT LOAN DEBT (ADD LINES 12 THROUGH 14)**			
16	**TOTAL FINANCIAL AID (ADD LINES 11 AND 15)**			
17	Expected Family Contribution (from your Student Aid Report)			
18	**TOTAL SELF-HELP (ADD LINES 16 AND 17 AND THEN SUBTRACT TOTAL FROM LINE 8)**			

CHAPTER 11 ACTION STEPS

❏ Start with a budget so that you don't get swept up by the process and end up taking on unfeasible debt.

❏ Don't get sticker shock. Just because the cost of attendance at a certain school is close to $50,000 does not mean that is what you will end up paying.

❏ Since need-aware colleges are harder to get into if you are applying for financial aid, B students who need aid also need more safety schools.

❏ Know the different types of financial aid forms and deadlines. There is a lot of paperwork in this process, so it's important to be organized.

❏ Search for private scholarships using the websites listed in this chapter. Make sure you qualify, keep track of deadlines, follow the rules for good essay writing, have it proofread, and watch out for scams!

❏ Avoid private loans if you can. However, if you really can't get around taking out a private student loan, borrow the bare minimum and research different loan companies instead of just going with your college's "preferred lender."

❏ Create a financial aid worksheet to determine the actual cost of attendance at each school to which you have been admitted once you receive your financial aid award letter.

CHAPTER 12

HOW PARENTS CAN HELP (AND HURT)

Note to students: Though the advice in this book is directed to you—the applicant— your parents are also heavily invested (both literally and figuratively) in your college application process. I wrote this chapter to help your parents understand how they can actively support you on your journey and how they can avoid doing things that might get in the way of your success. Feel free to read it and pass the information along, or just hand chapter 12 over to your parents while you work on implementing the advice in chapters 1 through 11.

Parents: You may think that applying to college is no big deal but it is important to be prepared for the challenges that come with this tricky rite of passage. It is the nexus of several anxieties rolled into one. We all want our children to be happy, successful, well-adjusted adults, and many parents picture the day that they drop their son or daughter off on a picturesque college campus as a major milestone in the fulfillment of this dream. At the same time, you'll be asking yourself lots of questions: *What if my teenager doesn't get into a good college? What if she sets her sights too high and gets her heart broken? What if he gets into his "dream school" and I can't afford it? How will we know if this is the right school for her? Will he do his schoolwork without me nagging him? Will she make the right decisions about her friends, her major, her career, her life? How can I keep him safe when he is away from home? What will our relationship be like once she leaves? What will the house feel like if he's not living there? Is my daughter leaving me for good? Am I about to lose my son?*

In all the years that I have worked with families, I have never met a parent who didn't have some anxiety concerning the college admissions process. It is a completely normal response to this challenging and uncertain transition. Give yourself permission to feel whatever you are feeling—frightened, anxious, guilty, excited, proud, or anything else. We can't change our emotions; the only thing we can control is how we respond to them. Some responses will be productive and can potentially help your child get into the college that is right for her. Others will be destructive and may put him at a disadvantage in the admissions process or, even worse, damage your relationship with your child. This chapter contains some do's and don'ts for parents who want to help their B students get into the college of their dreams.

HOW PARENTS CAN HELP B STUDENTS

I have seen many parents with nothing but love and good intentions drive their children crazy. Here are some things you can do to channel your nervous energy in a positive direction that will help your child succeed in the college application process.

DO LISTEN

Rationally, you know that your child is the one who will be going to college and this should be her decision; emotionally, it's hard to back off when you feel that she is about to make a big mistake, especially when you're paying for a chunk of it. Be forewarned that by the time the college search process is over, your teenager will have been bombarded with tons of advice, propaganda, and gossip. Information overload plus teenage emotions can often lead to silly conclusions. Your daughter becomes completely fixated on a particular college that she has never visited because "I love the school colors" or "My best friend is going there." Your son insists that he wants to go to a college across the country while you want him to stay within driving distance. She decides that she wants to major in African dance. He doesn't want to look at the state schools that are within your budget.

Working with families has taught me that one of the hardest things about the college search is that both students and parents feel a strong sense of ownership over the process, which inevitably leads to conflict. I've seen how frustrating it can be when the two parties come to the table with wildly different college lists or how hurt a mom can feel when her son flatly refuses to consider her beloved alma mater. Students want to live their lives and make their own decisions. Parents want to guide their children in the right direction. The fact that college sticker prices are in the hundreds of thousands of dollars just ratchets up the tension.

The best thing you can do to prevent these conflicts from blowing up into a full-on, unproductive war is to *listen*. Give your child room to consider different options and evaluate what really matters. When you sit down to discuss a college list, let your daughter speak first and absorb what she has to say before making your own suggestions. Instead of starting conversations by telling your son what to major in, what he is good at, or what he likes, let him feel that you acknowledge him and his autonomy. The best way to get your children to listen to you is by listening to them. You never know, they might just have something insightful to say!

DO GET YOUR FINANCIAL AID
FORMS IN ON TIME

In the college admissions process, there are certain things that only your child can do—like take the SATs or get a great grade on the final exam in his math class. There are also certain things that you as a parent can do—like take her on productive college visits or help him practice for his on-campus interviews. But one of the most important and helpful things you can do as a parent is to complete your financial aid forms on time. Unless your child is legally emancipated, you are responsible for helping to finance your child's higher education. The financial aid process can be time consuming and confusing. With so many families competing for financial aid, late applicants can be severely penalized. To maximize your child's chances of going to the college of her dreams, start your college financial planning early, get good information, stay organized, and get your financial aid forms in on time. This is simply not something that your child can do on her own.

DO HELP YOUR CHILD MEET DEADLINES

You may be lucky enough to have a child who can effortlessly juggle campus visits, high school course work, standardized tests, financial aid requirements, after-school commitments, and the all-important teenage social life. However, many parents will notice that their children start to become overwhelmed by responsibilities sometime in their junior year of high school. In frustration, many parents find themselves resorting to nagging: "Did you study your vocabulary words?" "Did you sign up for the marching band trip?" "Did you do your volunteer hours at the nursing home?" Anyone who has ever tried this technique knows that the typical teenage response is some version of "Get off my back" to be followed by further withdrawal of communication, which often starts the nagging cycle all over again.

The good news is that there is a better way to do things. Read the college admissions timeline in appendix A at the end of this book and set up a Google calendar with your child that you can both access. Doing this together and making the calendar public household knowledge creates a sense of accountability and also may give you a break from the daily nagging. As the year progresses, adjust the calendar so that the deadlines remain realistic. Avoid being so rigid that you abandon the calendar the first time a deadline goes unmet. The important thing is to be consistent about checking the calendar and using it as a guide.

If your child is open to it, you can also help him set up a spreadsheet with the various application components and supplementary essay questions that each college requires. This kind of organizational work may feel overwhelming to some teenagers who aren't used to paperwork; other teens may be just fine doing this on their own. The goal is to be helpful, not to take over. Use your judgment.

DO GET INFORMED

With so much information being thrown at your child, it can be easy to assume that she understands what is expected of her to get into the college of her dreams. Unfortunately, that is not always the case. High school guidance counselors come in many different shapes and sizes—from the obsessively driven, attentive, hands-on superhero to the overworked, checked-out, uninformed bureaucrat. Early on in the college process, make sure to meet with your child's counselor and see what kind of support her school gives.

QUESTIONS THAT PARENTS CAN ASK HIGH SCHOOL GUIDANCE COUNSELORS

- What is your personal philosophy in terms of supporting students through the college process?
- How often do you personally meet with students to advise them on the college process?
- Are there any resources at the school for scholarships or financial aid?
- Does the school have any data tools like Naviance that can give me information about where students with similar academic profiles have gone in the past?
- Do you help students with college essays?
- Does the school sponsor any campus visits?
- Do you recommend any other college-planning resources like books or websites?
- How do you work with the school's teachers to prepare teacher recommendations?
- When it comes to advising students on the high school courses that will best prepare them for college, do you offer recommendations or just let students decide what they should take?
- Do you ever call a college admissions officer to advocate for a student?
- Do you invite college admissions officers to the school to give information sessions? How can we find out when certain representatives will visit our high school?
- Do you recommend that we hire an independent college counselor to supplement the work that you will do at the school?

If so, do you have any recommendations? If we do hire an independent counselor, do you want to communicate with that counselor?

Once you assess how much support your child will get from his high school, you'll know how much you should be involved in helping him get good information about college. Reading this book is a great start. You can also check out some of the recommended websites and books in the Resource section. Students who have the best college outcomes tend to be actively engaged in seeking out good information about which colleges are best for them and what it takes to get in to these schools. Instead of assuming that your child will get everything he needs to know in school, encourage your child to get educated about the process and be hands-on.

DO VISIT CAMPUSES

With little to no independent travel experience, many high school students are intimidated by the prospect of planning college visits on their own. Enter Mom or Dad, travel agent extraordinaire. One way for you to take the pressure off and make sure that your child enjoys the benefits of campus visits is to offer to plan the trips. Early in junior year, sit down and ask your daughter where she might like to apply. If you find that she has already done research and has specific schools in mind, take out the calendar and discuss some good times to visit over the school year. If she responds to your questions with "I have no idea," don't be discouraged. You can still designate blocks of time in advance and fill in the particular schools later.

Once you are on campus, you will naturally have your own observations—you might pick up on the fact that, as a vegetarian, she will have a hard time finding things to eat in the cafeteria or that the college seems to be investing in their science labs instead of their theater, which could limit her options as a future actress. As hard as it may be, don't bombard your child with these comments until she has had a chance to form her own impression. Give her a little breathing room. Let her walk around by herself and take in the scenery. She might make interesting observations that you hadn't noticed. After all, there's no point in taking her on these college visits if yours is the only opinion that counts.

DO HELP WITH INTERVIEW PRACTICE A LITTLE AT A TIME

The best way for your child to prepare for a college interview is to practice answering questions about himself. Use the list of possible interview questions on pages 115–16 to help students get comfortable talking about things that they might never have considered before, like a favorite book or biggest weakness. Don't tackle the whole list at once. I find that cramming for an interview can backfire by overwhelming an already stressed-out teenager. Instead, if the moment is right and your child is receptive, ask a few questions over dinner, another few during a long drive, and a couple more when you're waiting at the doctor's office or standing in the supermarket checkout line. At first, don't offer too much feedback. Just let him get comfortable with the question-and-answer format and gain confidence. Once you see that he seems at ease with the interview process, you can offer some mild suggestions for specific answers to the practice questions. Ultimately, the biggest measure of a successful interview is whether or not your son comes across as genuine and at ease, so don't overdo the "coaching."

HOW PARENTS CAN HURT B STUDENTS

Now that you know how to help support your child through the application process, it is also important to understand common mistakes that parents make. Here are some things to avoid doing when it comes to college and financial aid admissions.

DON'T MAKE THE PROCESS ALL ABOUT YOU

I think 99 percent of the parents with whom I work have misused the word *we* at some point in the college application process. *We* want to apply early to the University of Maryland. *We're* thinking about taking AP Psychology next year. Will it look bad if *we* drop out of the marching band senior year? There's a difference between being involved in your child's educational choices and inserting yourself where you just don't belong. As difficult as it may seem, when it comes to college, it is really important to understand where your experience ends and your child's begins.

Making the college search process all about you can actually hurt your child's chances of finding and getting into her dream school. One of the worst things you can do as a parent is to try to relive your college experience by forcing your alma mater onto the list when it's not the best place for your child. Another common mistake to avoid is using your child to make up for your own feelings of inadequacy by pushing her into a college that you wanted to go to but couldn't. These are your dreams and experiences, not your child's.

To find a college that will allow them to thrive, students need to self-assess their academic and social priorities. Parents who can't see past themselves don't leave much room for their children to discover who they are and what they want. This not only results in students choosing the wrong colleges for bad reasons but also often leads to weaker applications. Overly self-centered parenting often produces children who are unable to identify and follow a genuine passion, write an essay with sincerity, or be comfortable in an interview. If you want your teenager to have the best possible college application, it is important to know when to back off.

DON'T CALL THE ADMISSIONS OFFICE

Every parent knows that raising children means supporting them through different stages of development. As hard as it is, there comes a time when you have to drop your kid off at school for the first time, let go of the bicycle handlebars, and get in the passenger seat next to your teenager behind the steering wheel. At some point, your child must become his own advocate instead of having you as his representative. If you haven't already encouraged this transition, now is the time.

Sometime between high school and college, parental involvement goes from being encouraged to frowned upon by the school. The terms

"Velcro parent" and "helicopter parent" have been coined by the media and widely used behind closed doors on college campuses to describe parents who are seen as being overly involved in every aspect of their children's lives—either by clinging to them directly or hovering above, ready to swoop in and rescue them when they meet a challenge. With the use of cell phones and the Internet for instant communication, many college students are in touch with their parents several times a day. Parental attachment has gotten so intense that many colleges are now introducing separation ceremonies into their orientation programs where Mom and Dad are encouraged to say good-bye and establish some boundaries that will allow their child to gain independence in college.

College students are legal adults who are expected to make their own decisions, be responsible for their actions, and engage with the outside world independently. The only time that colleges want to hear from parents is when tuition bills come due. Otherwise, they expect to deal with students themselves. Since the admissions process is the first time that a student communicates with a college, he needs to be the one doing the talking. After all, your child will be the one who will potentially enroll at this school. Colleges are very sensitive to parental overinvolvement on campus, and it is not in your child's best interest to leave the impression that he can't advocate for himself.

DON'T OVEREDIT YOUR CHILD'S COLLEGE ESSAY

A college application collects data from many different sources. There's a transcript, teacher recommendations, and guidance counselor recommendation, and some colleges even ask for a peer recommendation. The college essay is one of the only places where the applicant gets to express herself in her own words. This blank page should be artfully filled with genuine prose that adds something to the reader's understanding of who this person is and what she has to offer a college campus. Because of this, one of my main rules for college essay writing is that the essay should be written in the student's own voice. If your daughter dropped her college essay on the floor of her high school, a good friend should be able to identify that she wrote it even though the document does not have her name on it.

With so much riding on the college essay, I'm not suggesting that you completely disengage and let your child submit any old first draft to colleges. Naturally, you can help your child come up with a good topic that will "add" something to the rest of the college application (see chapter 8 for some useful college essay writing tips), give your feedback on drafts, and check for typos as well as grammatical errors. However, it is crucial that you resist the urge to overedit or insert your voice. I assure you that there are overwhelming odds that you will do your child a disservice by sitting down at the computer keyboard with good intentions.

During reading season, admissions officers spend months reading personal essays written by high school seniors. After investing *thousands* of hours reading teenage writing, it is pretty easy to spot something that is not written by a teenager. Parents tend to brag more about accomplishments, exaggerate the importance of certain events like getting an honorable mention at Model Congress, and gravitate toward topics like community service that they think will "look good on an application." Even if they don't change the subject matter, most parents write more formally and less personally than their children, which makes it easy for an experienced reader to detect certain words, phrases, references, or manners of speech that look out of place. If an admissions officer finds herself questioning the essay's authenticity, the essay is not going to help the applicant get into college. When it comes to personal statements, the key word is *personal*. So let your child do the writing and keep your hands to yourself.

DON'T BE AFRAID TO ASK FOR HELP WHEN YOU NEED IT

A decade of experience working with families has taught me the benefits of having a neutral third party to support both the parents and the student through the college application process. With so much invested in the outcome, almost everyone struggles with overwhelming nerves and emotions at some point. The future is uncertain. The pressure is on. It can be difficult to communicate. And sometimes we take out our frustrations on the people we love. Many students and parents find that the biggest challenge of applying to college has nothing to do with college—it has to do with family dynamics.

Studies have found that approximately 25 percent of all high school students now use an independent college counselor to help them with the application process. Fees for this service vary tremendously as does the quality of the counselor. If you do decide to hire someone, it's very important to investigate this person's credentials. (I personally prefer that independent counselors have experience reading applications in an admissions office, but there are exceptional former guidance counselors who are very educated about the process.) If you don't have a good recommendation from a friend, you can ask your guidance counselor or use the resources of accrediting organizations like the Independent Education Counselor Association (www.iecaonline.com) or the National Association of College Admissions and Financial Aid Counselors, or NACAC (www.nacacnet.org) for leads. Be sure to meet with as many candidates as necessary before you find someone whom both parents and student feel good about.

QUESTIONS TO ASK POTENTIAL INDEPENDENT COUNSELORS

- Have you ever read applications and made admissions decisions for a college?
- How many students have you advised?
- What is your success rate of college placement? How do you measure that?
- What percentage of your business is based on referrals from previous clients?
- How many college campuses have you visited in the past year?
- How do you approach ongoing professional development?
- How do you handle it when you come across a question that you don't know the answer to?
- What's your favorite part of your job?
- What's your least favorite part of your job?
- What aspects of the college admissions process do you advise students on?
- How do you include parents in the college admissions process?

Obviously, not everyone can afford to hire someone to provide individualized support for the college application process, especially with the cost of tuition looming on the horizon. Families working with a more modest budget can still find an agreed-upon third party to help offer advice, serve as a sounding board, or mitigate disputes. A cool aunt who has put three kids through college might have advice for planning campus visits. A well-read neighbor might be able to offer feedback on the college essay. Your accountant should be able to help you through the process of financial aid. You don't have to navigate the journey entirely on your own. If you find that you need help, ask for it.

ACTION STEPS FOR PARENTS

❑ Listen. The best way to get your child to listen to you is to listen to your child. Respect your teenager's opinions, even if they seem silly.

❑ Complete your financial aid forms on time. Your child doesn't have access to all the documents he needs for these applications, so this is one of the most important and helpful things you can do as a parent.

❑ Help your child stay organized with calendars and spreadsheets. Working on this together and making it public household knowledge may help your child meet deadlines without daily nagging.

❑ Visit colleges as a family. Take the reins on planning these visits as your teenager probably doesn't know much about reserving hotel rooms, booking transportation, or creating sensible itineraries.

❑ Practice the interview questions on pages 115–16. Ask a few questions at a time while you run errands or make dinner.

❏ Don't make it all about you. Unfortunately for some parents, you won't be bunking in the dorms or attending classes with your child, so let her have input in these important decisions.

❏ Don't assume that you will get all the college-planning information you need from school. Schedule a meeting with your child's guidance counselor and ask the questions in this chapter to learn more about the school's counseling program. Then supplement this information with other resources, if you need to.

❏ Don't call the admissions office or coaches. Colleges expect students to be their own advocates. Having Mom or Dad call on their behalf leaves a very negative impression.

❏ Don't overedit your child's essay. It's perfectly fine to read the essays to catch mistakes or offer feedback, but you must let your child's voice come through.

❏ Don't be afraid to ask for help when you need it. If you can afford an independent college counselor and think that you will benefit from it, do some research and ask the questions in this chapter.

APPENDIX A:

JUNIOR- AND SENIOR-YEAR COLLEGE ADMISSIONS TIMELINE

By now, you've probably surmised that applying to college is a complex *process*, not something that you can do in a day or even a month. Choosing a college that will allow you to thrive and putting together an outstanding application takes time; the process has many components, which can feel overwhelming at times. This appendix provides a timeline to help high school juniors and seniors understand what they should be doing for their college applications and when they should be doing it. Being organized and planning ahead goes a long way toward getting an email from a college admissions office congratulating you on your acceptance. Hopefully, you will learn a lot about yourself on the journey to your Dream U. Happy travels!

JUNIOR YEAR

SUMMER BEFORE 11TH GRADE
(JULY AND AUGUST)

TESTS

- Take a full-length practice SAT *and* a full-length practice ACT. Go to a library or another quiet place and time yourself on each section of the test. Be sure to use only real tests published by the College Board (SAT) or ACT Inc., not those published by companies like the Princeton Review or Kaplan.

- Use the results of these tests to make some preliminary decisions (you can always change your mind later) about which test you prefer to focus on.
- Research your test-prep options (see chapter 4 for suggestions).
- Start studying! I'm not suggesting that you spend your whole summer buried under prep books—just do a little at a time. The best way to study for standardized tests is to be consistent over time. I'm a big fan of forty-five- to sixty-minute study sessions five days a week.
- Create a "testing plan" for your SAT/ACT junior year. The SAT is offered in October, November, December, January, March, and May. The ACT is offered in September, October, December, February, April, and June. Try to give yourself three test dates in case you need to take the exam multiple times. Most colleges will use your "superscore," or the highest score on each section regardless of the test date, so there's little downside to taking the test a few times.
- Consider whether or not you plan to also take any SAT Subject Tests or AP exams. Students generally take these at the end of the school year, so factor these tests into your overall testing plan, if you decide to take them.
- If you have a learning disability, start researching and gathering materials to apply for College Board and/or ACT Inc. testing accommodations, if you haven't already.

EXTRACURRICULAR ACTIVITIES

- Without the pressure of school, summer is a great time to enhance your extracurricular profile. Fill your free time thoughtfully. Take a class, get an internship, work at a job, or explore your interests in a less conventional way. Just don't waste this time.

- Now is a good time to start making your priorities list as described in chapter 2. Think about the things that you want from a college and the things you need to thrive in the next stage of your life.
- Use your list to guide you as you begin to use online and print resources to learn more about colleges that could possibly be a good match for you.
- Although it's better to see colleges when classes are in session, if you have time this summer, think about visiting a few schools that interest you. Perhaps you can add some campus stops to your family vacation itinerary. Colleges offer tours and information sessions during the summer break.

FIRST SEMESTER (SEPTEMBER–DECEMBER)

ACADEMICS

- Meet with your guidance counselor to introduce yourself. Let him know that you are excited about college and welcome his suggestions. Find out about the college-planning resources offered at your school.
- Talk to your guidance counselor about your course schedule. Take the rigorous courses that you can reasonably do well in (that is, don't load up on too many honors and APs if you can't realistically get good grades in them). Unless you have a learning disability that makes it harder for you to do well in certain subjects, you should be taking English, history, math, science, and foreign language in your junior year, even if your high school does not require all of these courses.
- Get to know your teachers. You will likely ask one or two of them for recommendations. Keep any assignments or tests that you are proud of. You can reference them later in your teacher recommendation request letter.
- Contribute to class discussion. If you have a good idea, share it. Colleges want students who add something to their intellectual environment, so show your teachers (who will later be

recommending you) that you are prepared for and engaged in their classes.

- Focus on your schoolwork above all else. At the end of the day, you'll have more college options with better grades. Colleges look at grade trends, so make sure that you keep showing improvement as a student.

- Ask for help when you need it. Eleventh-grade courses can be very difficult. The difference between those who do well and those who do not often comes down to being able to let someone know when you don't understand the material. Many schools have free peer-tutoring programs, or you can ask your teacher or fellow students for some extra help to make sure that you understand the material.

- Know what is expected of you. I often hear about students who come home with bad grades even though they studied because they didn't know what was going to be tested. If you have a test or assignment coming up, be sure that you understand the teacher's expectations. When in doubt, just ask.

TESTS

- Take the PSATs (the practice SATs) and/or the PLAN (the practice ACT), if your school offers it. These practice tests are never sent to colleges so they are risk-free, helpful diagnostic tools. Use the results to inform your test-prep strategy.

- Continue to study for standardized tests; try to do forty-five to sixty minutes, five days a week. Consistency is key.

- Schedule a few full-length practice exams. In addition to learning the material, you need to build up your stamina.

- Sign up for tests that you plan to take next semester. If you sign up early, you are more likely to get a testing center close to home. The only thing worse than a four-hour test on a Saturday morning is waking up extra early to drive out to the testing center.

EXTRACURRICULAR ACTIVITIES

- Think quality over quantity. Hone in on a few activities or interests that you really enjoy. A surefire way to watch your grades suffer and lose your sanity is to take on too much outside of school.
- Find ways to show leadership and/or initiative. Make a contribution to the activities/clubs/hobbies that you do.

COLLEGE RESEARCH

- Continue to learn as much as you can about the colleges that might fit your priorities. In addition to using the Web and college guidebooks, be sure to talk to students and alumni.
- Junior fall is a great time for campus visits. Classes are now in session and students are back on campus. Try to meet up with a real student when you visit, even if she's your third cousin twice removed. Sign in at the admissions office, even if you don't take a formal tour or go to an information session. Also, take notes about the *specific* things that you liked about a campus, which you can use later for your college essays.

SECOND SEMESTER (JANUARY–JUNE)

ACADEMICS

- Continue your good work from last semester: study hard, contribute to class, ask for help when you need it, and make sure that you understand the teacher's expectations.
- Continue to keep assignments and tests that you are proud of, which you can reference in your teacher recommendation request letters.
- Choose your senior-year courses. Colleges really want to see that you are challenging yourself and growing as a student during high school. As a senior, I recommend that you take English, history, science, math, and foreign language (unless you have a learning disability that makes this course load unrealistic). You can specialize later on, but all educated people should know something about each of these subjects. In terms of honors and AP courses, enroll in as many rigorous classes as you

can reasonably handle, but don't set yourself up for disaster by taking on too much.

TESTS

- Second semester of junior year is crunch time for standardized tests. Some students take them as early as January, others wait until March or May to take their first SAT. I wouldn't recommend waiting longer—unless there are special circumstances—because you may not be giving yourself enough time to retake the test before your college applications are due.
- If you've been pacing yourself and studying consistently, continue to do so. You can't cram for these tests, but you can prepare for them.
- Schedule more frequent full-length, timed practice tests to build up your test-taking stamina. It's always good to take them on a weekend morning to simulate the testing conditions you'll encounter on the big day.
- If you are taking SAT Subject Tests or AP exams, be sure to prepare. The College Board website (www.CollegeBoard.org) has one free practice exam in each subject, so take advantage of that.
- Don't give up! If you get a score that you are unhappy with, try again. Colleges will "superscore" your test results, so commit yourself to doing well even if you have to take the test up to three times. (By the third time, you've probably done as well as you can, so call it a day.)

EXTRACURRICULAR ACTIVITIES

- Now is a good time to begin a rough draft of your accomplishments doc. Look at how you spend your time outside of class and reflect on how you can use the upcoming summer and fall to build on the things that you are already doing in interesting ways.
- Plan for the summer. Arrangements for courses, jobs, internships, and other activities need to be made in the spring.

- Be a leader. Many school clubs hold elections for the following year's leadership positions in the spring. Nominate and advocate for yourself.

COLLEGE RESEARCH

- Set up a meeting with your guidance counselor to talk about your preliminary college list. Your guidance counselor may come up with a very different list than you expected, so keep an open mind but also remember that your guidance counselor is only one of several sources of information. You don't have to apply to every school that your counselor suggests or eliminate colleges that are not on your counselor's list.
- If you are considering working with an independent college adviser, you should interview and select a consultant before the end of the year.
- Great times for college visits include Martin Luther King Day, February break, and spring break. These are good opportunities to see campuses with students and sit in on some classes. Prioritize any schools to which you might consider applying early.
- Attend college fairs and information sessions for the schools that you really like. Get admissions officers' business cards and follow up with a polite email to introduce yourself, ask questions, or state your interest in their schools.

SENIOR YEAR

SUMMER BEFORE 12TH GRADE
(JULY AND AUGUST)

TESTS

- Continue to study for any standardized tests that you hope to take in the fall. You still have some test dates left before your applications are due.

Important Test Dates

	LAST TEST DATE BEFORE EARLY DECISION/EARLY ACTION	LAST TEST DATE BEFORE REGULAR DECISION
SAT	October of senior year	December of senior year (for most selective colleges that have an early January deadline; but many less selective colleges have later deadlines, so check with individual schools)
ACT	September of senior year	December of senior year (again, some less selective schools may accept the later tests, so be sure to check)

EXTRACURRICULAR ACTIVITIES

- Now is the time to pursue something thoughtful that builds on your genuine interests and adds to the overall picture of how you can contribute to the college of your dreams.
- Complete your accomplishments doc. You can give this to your counselor or bring it with you on interviews. You can also attach it to your application to enhance your extracurricular profile.

COLLEGE RESEARCH

- Continue to refine your list according to your priorities. Use Naviance as a tool to guide you in selecting reach, target, and safety schools, now that you have some standardized test scores.
- Visit any campuses that you are considering applying early to. Schedule interviews at colleges that offer them on-campus.
- For your top-choice colleges, find out who your regional admissions officer is and if that person will be coming to your area to give an information session in the fall.

COLLEGE APPLICATIONS

- Prepare for any on-campus interviews using the advice in chapter 7. Send thank-you notes by mail to anyone who interviewed you.

- Work on your Common Application essays in July.
- Set up your Common Application account on August 1.
- Once they are available, make a spreadsheet with all the supplementary essay questions that you will have to answer. Consider how you can use the same essay topic to answer multiple questions. Start working on your supplements for your early decision/early action schools.
- Prepare any materials you need for your guidance counselor and teacher recommendations.

FIRST SEMESTER (SEPTEMBER–DECEMBER)

COLLEGE APPLICATIONS: SEPTEMBER AND OCTOBER

- Meet with your guidance counselor and teacher(s) to discuss recommendations. Give them documents that you have prepared over the summer to help enhance the recommendations. Let them know which schools you plan to apply early to and what the deadlines are.
- Make sure you have at least two adults read your Common Application essays independently. Also ask one or two friends to read them and answer this question: "Does this sound like me?"
- Continue to work on your early decision/early action supplements. Send them in a few days before the deadline, if you can.
- Prepare for any on-campus or alumni interviews. Practice interview questions and stay informed about current events. Send thank-you notes (not emails) after interviews.
- Prepare any supplementary materials—art portfolio, music recording, and so on.
- Attend any local information sessions for the colleges on your list. Meet your regional admissions officer and send a follow-up email to say that you enjoyed the presentation and plan to apply.
- Request that transcripts be sent to all the colleges on your list.
- Write thank-you notes to anyone who has written you a recommendation.

- Check with your early decision/early action schools to make sure that your application is complete.
- Work on your regular decision supplements. *Do not leave these for the last minute.* The only thing worse than getting deferred or rejected from your early decision/early action schools is scrambling to write a bunch of essays at the last minute over the Christmas break. Aim to have *all* college essays complete by December 15.

COLLEGE APPLICATIONS: DECEMBER

- Many early decision schools will reply in mid- to late December, so congratulations if you get accepted! If you get deferred, call your regional admissions officer and ask for more information about how to improve your chances of being admitted in the spring. This is also a good opportunity to reiterate your interest in attending this college, despite being deferred.
- Finish your regular decision supplementary essays.
- Make sure all your regular decision applications are submitted in advance of the deadline.

ACADEMICS

- First-semester senior-year grades count. Focus on your courses so that you can leave the admissions office with the best possible impression of your academic trajectory.

TESTS

- Send your official scores to the colleges on your list from the College Board or ACT Inc.
- Finish taking any standardized tests you need to complete senior year *before* the early or regular decision deadlines.

EXTRACURRICULAR ACTIVITIES

- Make your senior year count. If you have a leadership position, use it to make an impact on your high school. Mentor other students. Share your knowledge.

SECOND SEMESTER (JANUARY–JUNE)

COLLEGE ADMISSIONS

- Submit any remaining applications with January or February deadlines.
- Make sure that your high school sends your first-semester grades to all the colleges on your list.
- Check with your regular decision schools to make sure that your application is complete.
- If you have been deferred from an early decision/early action school:
  - > Write an update letter (see pages 86–88).
  - > Ask for an additional recommendation from a senior-year teacher.
  - > Ask your counselor to follow up with a phone call to the regional admissions officer to reiterate your interest in the school.
  - > If you know any active alumni of this particular school, ask them to advocate for you.
- Once you have been accepted to your regular decision colleges:
  - > Visit all the schools that you are considering, if you haven't already.
  - > Once you select the college that you plan to attend, accept their offer of admission in writing and by sending a deposit by the deadline. If you miss the deadline, the offer may be rescinded.

ACADEMICS

- Although colleges do not make admissions decisions based on second-semester grades, they do review your final grades before you are able to matriculate. Any obvious drops can have serious consequences, so don't fall victim to senioritis and don't blow off your classes!

APPENDIX B:

GETTING INTO A TOP COLLEGE
THROUGH THE SIDE DOOR

Let's get real for a minute. You're reading this book because you're not a "perfect" student. Your transcript doesn't have rows of beaming As and your SAT scores probably didn't break any school records. Many college admissions advisers are going to look at your transcript and tell you that you have no shot at an Ivy League college. Others are going to try to enlighten you with convincing arguments that you wouldn't want to go to those schools even if you did get in.

Loren Pope's popular books, *Looking Beyond the Ivy League: Finding the College That's Right for You* and *Colleges That Change Lives: 40 Schools You Should Know About Even If You're Not a Straight-A Student*, make a persuasive case for the merits of less selective liberal arts colleges that specialize in undergraduate education. He argues that the contact you have with professors and the support you receive from your campus community is far more important than whether you go to a college that is highly ranked by *U.S. News & World Report*. Pope doesn't just rely on anecdotes to extol the virtues of his forty "life-changing" schools; he backs up his argument with important statistics, like solid graduation and employment rates, at the small liberal arts colleges that he highlights. His books are so popular that the forty colleges he endorsed have since adopted Pope's branding, creating the Colleges That Change Lives website (www.ctcl.org) and giving joint admissions presentations to prospective students.

If you learn best when you know your teachers and who prefers collaboration over competition with your peers, Pope's list is a great place to start searching for your Dream U. But what if you feel suffocated in small classrooms and isolated on rural campuses? What if you are so passionate about a particular subject or career that you would rather focus on in-depth study instead of a broad liberal arts education? What if you want to go to a college with name recognition?

The problem with Pope's approach is that it disregards the wide range of considerations that students make when looking at colleges. Considering the astronomical cost of college, more students and their families are coming to see college as an *investment*, a credential that they need to succeed in any career path they choose. They don't just want their college experience to open their minds—they want their college to open doors to employment and graduate school after graduation. These are the brand-name shoppers that I described earlier.

If you are a brand-name shopper, I have good news for you. Even if you are not at the top of your class, you can still go to an Ivy League school. Some of the country's most selective colleges have alternative undergraduate programs with more relaxed admissions criteria. Some of these programs are geared toward nontraditional students—adults who took time off between high school and college or military veterans who want to enroll in college after their service. Others offer a more supportive learning environment for students who are transitioning from high school with less-than-perfect grades but still have a lot to offer. All of the programs in this chapter will consider high school students with some blemishes on their academic record and lead to a bachelor's degree from a prestigious college.

PROGRAMS GEARED TOWARD TRADITIONAL COLLEGE STUDENTS WHO ENROLL IMMEDIATELY AFTER HIGH SCHOOL

The following programs are designed for promising high school students who may need a little extra academic support before entering a rigorous college environment. These are two-year programs that offer smaller classes that emphasize academic skill building. Students who successfully complete these programs are then granted admission to other undergraduate programs within the institutions (for example, the College of Arts and Sciences) and graduate with the same bachelor's degree as their peers.

COLLEGE OF GENERAL STUDIES AT BOSTON UNIVERSITY

The College of General Studies at Boston University (BU) was created for high school students who needed a little more support in transitioning to college. General Studies students spend their first two years at BU in smaller, interdisciplinary classes that are focused on building academic skills and relationships with faculty and peers. After two years, students with at least a 2.3 GPA will be able to continue in one of the other nine undergraduate schools at BU and graduate after four years with a bachelor's degree in their choice of major. Students in the College of General Studies can live on campus and study abroad; the school seeks to create a very intimate sense of community for undergraduates.

ADMISSIONS REQUIREMENTS
The admissions process for the College of General Studies is similar to the regular undergraduate admissions process except that it is less selective. The average General Studies student has a class rank in the top 21 percent, a 3.3 GPA, an SAT score of 1785 or a 26 on the ACT (compared to students admitted to the other BU undergraduate

programs who are in the top 10 percent of their high school classes, have an average GPA of 3.6, a 1966 on the SAT or a 29 on the ACT).

PROS

- Geared toward traditional high school students.
- Seeks to build a strong community for students who need some extra support.
- Emphasizes academic skill building for college, which makes it ideal for students who want a more nurturing academic environment.
- Less selective than other BU programs.
- After two years at General Studies, students can transfer to any other undergraduate program at BU and graduate in four years.

CONS

- Though need-based financial aid is available, the General Studies program costs the same as other undergraduate programs at BU, which is one of the most expensive private colleges in the country.
- Limited academic flexibility in the first two years; students are required to take three integrated liberal arts courses each semester.

CONTACT INFORMATION

College of General Studies
Boston University
871 Commonwealth Avenue
Boston, MA 02215
617-353-2850
www.bu.edu/cgs/contact-us

OXFORD COLLEGE AT EMORY UNIVERSITY

Oxford College is a small, intensive liberal arts college at Emory University that is designed to nurture students' personal and academic development in the first two years of college. Oxford is geared to high school students who need a little extra support in their transition to college. Students spend their first two years living on and taking classes at the Oxford College campus in Oxford, Georgia (thirty-five miles from the main Emory campus in Atlanta). Then they are automatically enrolled at the Emory College of Arts and Sciences in Atlanta for their last two years, or they may apply to Emory's undergraduate business or nursing schools. Because Oxford is focused on community and academic skill building, students are required to live on campus and take seminar-style classes together.

ADMISSIONS REQUIREMENTS
Students may apply directly to Oxford College while in high school. The admissions process is less selective than at Emory's other undergraduate programs. Oxford accepts 44 percent of applicants compared with a 27 percent acceptance rate for Emory College.

PROS
- Small classes where students are encouraged to get to know their peers and professors.
- Focus on community building.
- Less selective admissions process than other Emory schools.
- Guaranteed transfer to Emory College of Arts and Sciences after two years.

CONS
- Oxford College is thirty-five miles away from the main Emory campus. Students may feel separated from sporting events and other mainstream campus traditions.
- The Oxford College curriculum is very rigid, which means that students have limited academic flexibility.
- Though need-based financial aid is available, Oxford College costs the same as other undergraduate programs at Emory, which is one of the most expensive private colleges in the country.

Oxford College of Emory University
100 Hamill Street
Oxford, GA 30054
770-784-8888
http://oxford.emory.edu

NEW YORK UNIVERSITY'S CORE
PROGRAM IN LIBERAL STUDIES

The Core Program in Liberal Studies at NYU is designed to provide an intimate environment with an interdisciplinary academic focus for students who would benefit from a more supportive classroom environment to help them transition to college. This two-year program offers seminar-style classes and focuses on building fundamental interdisciplinary skills that all students need to succeed in college; in addition to core courses, first-year students can select one elective course each semester; sophomores get to choose two elective courses each semester. Students who have completed the two-year program with at least a 2.0 GPA can transition into one of NYU's other undergraduate programs where they can complete their bachelor's degrees. Core students tend to be recent high school graduates. They may live on the NYU campus and study abroad.

ADMISSIONS REQUIREMENTS

The Core Program application process is similar to that of the other undergraduate programs at NYU. The university does not officially release acceptance rates for various undergraduate programs, but an admissions officer told me that the Core Program is less selective; admissions officers generally accept students who are on the edge of gaining admission to one of NYU's other undergraduate programs but come up just a bit short.

PROS
- Students may enroll directly after high school and are fully integrated into the NYU undergraduate community.

- Intimate interdisciplinary seminars help students make a smooth transition from high school and build the skills they need to succeed in college.
- Admission to the Core Program is less selective than admission to other undergraduate programs.

CONS

- The Core Program has rigid academic requirements; students have limited course options in their first two years.
- Though need-based financial aid is available, the Core Program costs the same as other undergraduate programs at NYU, which is one of the most expensive private colleges in the country.

CONTACT INFORMATION

Liberal Studies: The Core Program
New York University
665 Broadway, 11th Floor
New York, NY 10012
212-998-7259
core.info@nyu.edu
www.core.ls.nyu.edu

PROGRAMS GEARED TOWARD NONTRADITIONAL STUDENTS

The programs in this section are generally geared toward "nontraditional" students; these students are not enrolling immediately after high school. They tend to be older than "traditional" students (those who enroll immediately after high school). Many of them work during the day and support themselves instead of being dependent on their parents. Despite this, some brand-name shoppers will find these programs attractive because they lead to bachelor's degrees from prestigious universities like Harvard and Columbia and don't have the same rigid selection criteria. They also tend to be less expensive than the "traditional" program at the same private college.

HARVARD EXTENSION SCHOOL

The Harvard Extension School offers a bachelor's degree in liberal arts with the option to pursue one of twenty different fields of study (similar to a major). Although high school students may apply for enrollment immediately after graduation, the Extension School primarily serves nontraditional students. The average student age is thirty-three and students are not permitted to live on campus, so don't expect a "traditional" college experience. Courses are offered evenings, Saturdays, and online. Students can study abroad for credit during the summer months, and it is possible to graduate in four years, though most Extension students take longer to complete their degrees because they work full-time.

ADMISSIONS REQUIREMENTS
Before you are eligible to apply, you must achieve B or higher in three preadmission courses. These credits can be taken online while you are still in high school and do count toward your degree. Once you complete these courses, you can then fill out an application. SAT scores are not required for admission.

PROS
- Students can earn a bachelor's degree from Harvard University without having good high school grades or SAT scores (as long as you meet the other admissions criteria).
- At $995 to $1,175 per course, the Extension School is much more affordable than a degree from Harvard College (the "traditional" undergraduate school at Harvard). A four-year education might cost you as little as $35,000 (not including room and board), and students can apply for need-based financial aid.
- Harvard Extension School offers over two hundred online courses and students are only required to take sixteen credits on campus. Students have much more flexibility over their

schedule and residency options than in a traditional bachelor's degree program.

- Students take courses with real Harvard professors and have access to the Harvard resources, such as the library and career counseling services.

CONS

- Because Extension students do not live in dorms, students may not feel like they are part of the Harvard undergraduate community. You'll have to live in an off-campus apartment, cook for yourself, and do your own cleaning.
- As a recent high school graduate, you will be taking courses with students who are much older than you. It may be difficult to relate to classmates who work part-time and have responsibilities associated with adulthood like caring for families or making mortgage payments.

CONTACT INFORMATION

Havard Extension School
51 Brattle Street
Cambridge, MA 02138
617-495-9413
www.extension.harvard.edu

COLUMBIA UNIVERSITY SCHOOL OF GENERAL STUDIES

High school students who are willing to take a year off after graduation are eligible to apply to the School of General Studies at Columbia University—a side door to an elite education at one of the most selective colleges in the world. General Studies was founded for nontraditional students, and the average age of the student body is twenty-nine. However, unlike some other programs geared toward older students, those enrolled at General Studies can take classes with the entire Columbia University undergraduate community and live in university housing. The cost of full-time enrollment is the same as Columbia's other undergraduate programs and need-based financial aid is available to qualified students.

ADMISSIONS REQUIREMENTS

The School of General Studies requires a fairly traditional application with high school transcripts, standardized test scores, recommendations, and a personal statement. Admissions officers recommend a high school GPA of 3.0 or higher, though they will consider other nontraditional candidates (even those with a GED instead of a high school diploma) who show potential.

PROS

- Students are integrated into regular Columbia undergraduate courses.
- Students are eligible to live in university housing.
- Though admission is selective, the School of General Studies is less selective than Columbia's other undergraduate programs.
- The School of General Studies will consider nontraditional students who have GEDs instead of high school diplomas.

CONS

- High school students must wait at least one year after graduation to apply for admission.

CONTACT INFORMATION

Columbia University School of General Studies
408 Lewisohn Hall, MC4101
2970 Broadway
New York, NY 10027
212-854-2772
http://gs.columbia.edu

UNIVERSITY OF PENNSYLVANIA COLLEGE OF LIBERAL AND PROFESSIONAL STUDIES

The College of Liberal and Professional Studies (LPS) at Penn is geared toward nontraditional students who seek a degree from this prestigious Ivy League university with a flexible schedule. (*Note:* Most students are enrolled part-time). LPS students can take regular undergraduate courses at Penn as well as special weekend and evening courses. LPS offers over fifty different majors and will allow almost half of the credits for the bachelor's degree to be taken at another institution (which makes this a terrific program for transfer students). The Penn admissions office emphasizes that LPS is a program for nontraditional students and cautions high school students from approaching this program as an alternative route to the University of Pennsylvania; students under twenty-one years old are only allowed to enroll part-time. Still, they will consider younger students with at least a 3.0 GPA and a good reason to study part-time.

ADMISSIONS REQUIREMENTS

High school graduates or current college students with at least a 3.0 GPA will be seriously considered for admissions. Students under the age of twenty-one are required to contact the admissions office for an interview as this program is geared toward nontraditional, adult students. Students who have been rejected from another undergraduate program at the University of Pennsylvania must wait one year before applying for admission to LPS. Though the admissions committee considers students' academic records, they also look closely at academic potential and personal motivation to make a contribution to the Penn community.

PROS

- Lots of academic flexibility in terms of scheduling and majors offered.
- Students can take regular Penn courses and are eligible for on-campus housing.

- The LPS admissions process puts much less emphasis on high school academic record than the other undergraduate programs at the University of Pennsylvania.
- SAT scores are not required for admission.
- The LPS program is approximately $75,000 cheaper than a traditional Penn bachelor's degree (based on four-year estimates from the 2011–12 school year).
- The LPS program allows for almost half of the courses for the bachelor's degree to be taken at another undergraduate institution, which makes it a great option for transfer students.

CONS

- This program is expressly geared toward nontraditional students; applicants under twenty-one may only study part-time and are generally discouraged from applying.
- Most LPS students take courses part-time, so it might be difficult to feel a sense of community.

CONTACT INFORMATION

University of Pennsylvania
The College of Liberal and Professional Studies
3440 Market Street, Suite 100
Philadelphia, PA 19104-3335
215-898-7326
www.sas.upenn.edu/lps

GEORGETOWN UNIVERSITY SCHOOL OF CONTINUING STUDIES

Georgetown's School of Continuing Studies is designed for nontraditional students (the average age is thirty-five) who want a selective college experience with flexible and convenient classes. To receive a bachelor's degree in liberal studies, students are required to take thirteen core courses, ten of which are interdisciplinary and focus on the evolution of Western civilization. In addition, students choose from fourteen different concentrations (similar to majors) or design an "individualized study" plan. To accommodate working professionals, classes are held on evenings or weekends, though students may take a limited number of electives at one of Georgetown's other undergraduate programs. The program also offers academic skill-building opportunities for students through advisers, mentors, and the resources at the Academic Writing Center. Students are not eligible for on-campus housing and cannot apply immediately after high school; they must take at least one year off.

ADMISSIONS REQUIREMENTS

The School of Continuing Studies accepts about half of the students who apply. High school transcripts (or a GED certificate), two letters of recommendation, and a three-page essay are required, but the admissions committee does not require SAT scores.

PROS

- The School of General Studies is much less selective than Georgetown's other undergraduate programs (50 percent acceptance rate compared with only 18 percent in 2012).
- SAT scores are not required for admission.
- Tuition is less expensive. Based on the numbers for 2012–13, tuition for a Continuing Studies student amounts to about $108,000 for all bachelor's degree courses—about $65,000 less than four years of tuition at Georgetown's other undergraduate programs.

CONS

- The program is designed for nontraditional students. The average age of students is thirty-five and applicants may not apply directly from high school.
- Students may not live on campus, which makes it difficult to feel a sense of community.
- With thirteen core course requirements, some students may find the curriculum too restrictive.

Georgetown University
School of Continuing Studies
Office of Admissions
3307 M Street NW, Suite 202
Washington, DC 20007
202-687-8700
http://scs.georgetown.edu

TULANE SCHOOL OF CONTINUING STUDIES

Originally founded as an outreach program for local teachers in 1866, the School of Continuing Studies (SCS) at Tulane has greatly expanded and now offers a variety of undergraduate courses and majors in its bachelor's degree program. Though students may apply to SCS directly after high school, 60 percent are over twenty-five. With flexible online, night, and weekend course options, most students attend part-time because they are local, working adults (70 percent are New Orleans residents). SCS students may live on campus, buy a meal plan, participate in campus organizations, and study abroad. However, they are restricted to taking courses in the School of Continuing Studies.

ADMISSIONS REQUIREMENTS

The School of Continuing Studies has an open enrollment policy. They accept anyone with a high school diploma or a GED and do not require standardized test scores, essays, or recommendations.

PROS

- Open enrollment at a selective university! No test scores, essays, or high school GPA requirements.
- Students may apply directly from high school.
- Less expensive than a traditional Tulane undergraduate degree. Based on 2011–12 fees, students can take all the courses they need to graduate with a bachelor's degree for $36,240, which is about $9,000 less than one year of tuition at Tulane's five other undergraduate schools.
- Students may live on campus and study abroad.

CONS

- Students may only take classes at the School of Continuing Studies.
- Most students are local adults who are enrolled part-time; a full-time, traditional student may have a hard time relating to classmates.

CONTACT INFORMATION

Tulane University School of Continuing Studies
6823 St. Charles Avenue
New Orleans, LA 70118
504-865-5555
www.scs.tulane.edu

APPENDIX C:

A LIST OF COLLEGES WORTH CONSIDERING

The following list of schools is designed to help you get started on your journey toward finding the colleges that will meet your priorities and truly allow you to thrive. I selected these colleges and universities based on admissions rates and average academic credentials for admitted students. However, these are by no means the *only* colleges that B students should consider. Please use this list as one of many tools in your college search. (See chapter 2 for additional resources that will help you find your Dream U.)

Northeastern Colleges and Universities

COLLEGE	LOCATION	UNDERGRADUATE ENROLLMENT
Allegheny College	Meadville, PA	2,100 (medium)
American University	Washington, DC	7,200 (medium)
Bard College	Annandale on Hudson, NY	2,000 (small)
Boston University	Boston, MA	18,600 (large)
Brandeis University	Waltham, MA	3,500 (medium)
Bryn Mawr College	Bryn Mawr, PA	1,300 (small)
Clark University	Worcester, MA	2,300 (medium)
College of the Holy Cross	Worcester, MA	2,900 (medium)
Connecticut College	New London, CT	1,900 (small)
Drexel University	Philadelphia, PA	15,000 (medium)
Fordham University	New York, NY	8,400 (medium)

SIX-YEAR GRADUATION RATE	ADMISSIONS RATE	AVERAGE SAT/ACT SCORES (25TH–75TH PERCENTILE)
80%	58%	1300
77%	42%	1170–1370
77%	35%	1350–1420
85%	49%	1180–1370
91%	40%	1230–1450
87%	46%	1200–1430
80%	68%	1080–1310
91%	33%	1210–1380
84%	34%	1250–1410
NA	58%	1100–1310
NA	42%	1150–1340

COLLEGE	LOCATION	UNDERGRADUATE ENROLLMENT
Franklin and Marshall College	Lancaster, PA	2,400 (medium)
George Washington University	Washington, DC	10,400 (medium)
Hampshire College	Amherst, MA	1,500 (small)
Juniata College	Huntingdon, PA	1,600 (small)
Lehigh University	Bethlehem, PA	4,900 (medium)
Marlboro College	Marlboro, VT	270 (small)
Mount Holyoke	South Hadley, MA	2,400 (medium)
Muhlenberg College	Allentown, PA	2,500 (medium)
New York University	New York, NY	22,300 (large)
Northeastern University	Boston, MA	16,400 (large)
Pennsylvania State University	University Park, PA	39,000 (large)
Rensselaer Polytech Institute	Troy, NY	5,300 (medium)
Rutgers – The State University of New Jersey	Piscataway, NJ	31,300 (large)
Skidmore College	Saratoga Springs, NY	2,700 (medium)
Smith College	Northampton, MA	2,600 (medium)
St. Lawrence University	Canton, NY	2,400 (medium)
Stevens Institute of Technology	Hoboken, NJ	2,400 (medium)
Syracuse University	Syracuse, NY	14,700 (medium)
Trinity College	Hartford, CT	2,300 (medium)
Union College	Schenectady, NY	2,200 (medium)
University of Connecticut	Storrs, CT	17,800 (large)
University of Delaware	Newark, DE	17,100 (large)
University of Massachusetts	Amherst, MA	21,800 (large)
University of Pittsburg	Pittsburgh, PA	18,400 (large)
University of Rochester	Rochester, NY	5,600 (medium)
University of Vermont	Burlington, VT	11,500 (medium)
Ursinus College	Collegeville, PA	1,800 (small)
Wellesley College	Wellesley, MA	2,500 (medium)
Yeshiva University	New York, NY	2,800 (medium)

SIX-YEAR GRADUATION RATE	ADMISSIONS RATE	AVERAGE SAT/ACT SCORES (25TH–75TH PERCENTILE)
85%	39%	1240–1390
81%	33%	1210–1380
63%	71%	1350
76%	71%	1280
87%	33%	1220–1440
64%	87%	NA
85%	52%	1200–1420
86%	43%	1120–1340
86%	33%	1260–1460
77%	35%	1250–1430
87%	52%	1090–1300
82%	40%	1290–1470
77%	61%	1080–1310
84%	42%	1150–1350
85%	46%	1200–1400
80%	43%	1150–1320
79%	42%	1190–1390
NA	49%	1050–1270
86%	30%	1180–1368
86%	43%	1200–1380
83%	47%	1130–1310
78%	58%	1100–1300
67%	66%	1090–1280
NA	58%	1170–1380
85%	34%	1230–1440
72%	75%	1090–1280
80%	70%	1320
92%	31%	1290--1490
77%	69%	1090–1360

West Coast Colleges and Universities

COLLEGE	LOCATION	UNDERGRADUATE ENROLLMENT
Brigham Young University	Provo, UT	30,700 (large)
The Evergreen State College	Olympia, WA	4,500 (medium)
Lewis and Clark College	Portland, OR	2,100 (medium)
Mills College	Oakland, CA	940 (small)
Occidental College	Los Angeles, CA	2,100 (medium)
Pepperdine University	Malibu, CA	3,500 (medium)
Reed College	Portland, OR	1,500 (small)
Saint Mary's College of California	Moraga, CA	3,000 (medium)
Scripps College	Claremont, CA	970 (small)
University of California – Davis	Davis, CA	25,100 (large)
University of California – Irvine	Irvine, CA	22,000 (large)
University of California – San Diego	San Diego, CA	23,000 (large)
University of California – Santa Barbara	Santa Barbara, CA	18,600 (large)
University of California – Santa Cruz	Santa Cruz, CA	15,900 (large)
University of Colorado – Boulder	Boulder, CO	36,300 (large)
University of Denver	Denver, CO	5,400 (medium)
University of Puget Sound	Tacoma, WA	2,700 (medium)
University of San Diego	San Diego, CA	5,500 (medium)
University of Washington	Seattle, WA	29,000 (large)
Whitman College	Walla Walla, WA	1,600 (small)
Willamette University	Salem, OR	2,100 (small)

SIX-YEAR GRADUATION RATE	ADMISSIONS RATE	AVERAGE SAT/ACT SCORES (25TH–75TH PERCENTILE)
78%	63%	26–30
NA	96%	1220
75%	66%	1190–1380
57%	57%	1280
84%	38%	1200–1380
81%	32%	1100–1330
79%	40%	1300–1470
61%	NA	NA
88%	36%	1450
82%	46%	1090–1340
NA	48%	1060–1310
81%	36%	1110–1360
79%	46%	1120–1360
73%	67%	1020–1270
68%	87%	24–28
79%	68%	25–30
73%	52%	1340
75%	48%	1130–1320
NA	58%	1080–1350
85%	54%	1250–1440
77%	57%	1320

Midwestern Colleges and Universities

COLLEGE	LOCATION	UNDERGRADUATE ENROLLMENT
Antioch University	Yellow Springs, OH	140 (small)
Beloit College	Beloit, WI	1,400 (small)
Carleton College	Northfield, MN	2,000 (medium)
Carnegie Mellon University	Pittsburgh, PA	6,300 (medium)
Case Western Reserve University	Cleveland, OH	4,000 (medium)
College of Wooster	Wooster, OH	2,000 (small)
Cornell College	Mount Vernon, IA	1,200 (small)
Denison College	Granville, OH	2,300 (medium)
DePauw College	Greencastle, IN	2,400 (medium)
Earlham College	Richmond, IN	1,100 (small)
Grinnell College	Grinnell, IA	1,700 (small)
Hillsdale College	Hillsdale, MI	1,400 (small)
Hiram College	Hiram, OH	1,300 (small)
Hope College	Holland, MI	3,300 (medium)
Illinois Wesleyan University	Bloomington, IL	2,100 (medium)
Kalamazoo College	Kalamazoo, MI	1,400 (small)
Kenyon College	Gambier, OH	1,700 (small)
Knox College	Galesburg, IL	1,400 (small)
Lawrence University	Appleton, WI	1,500 (small)
Macalester College	St. Paul, MN	2,000 (small)
Michigan State University	East Lansing, MI	36,700 (large)
Oberlin College	Oberlin, OH	3,000 (medium)
Ohio State – Columbus	Columbus, OH	42,900 (large)
Ohio Wesleyan University	Delaware, OH	1,800 (small)
Purdue University – West Lafayette	West Lafayette, IN	30,800 (large)
St. Louis University	St. Louis, MO	8,700 (medium)
St. Olaf College	Northfield, MN	3,200 (medium)
University of Illinois – Urbana-Champaign	Champaign, IL	32,300 (large)
University of Iowa	Iowa City, IA	21,600 (large)
University of Michigan – Ann Arbor	Ann Arbor, MI	27,400 (large)

SIX-YEAR GRADUATION RATE	ADMISSIONS RATE	AVERAGE SAT/ACT SCORES (25TH–75TH PERCENTILE)
NA	NA	NA
76%	71%	1350
93%	31%	1510
87%	30%	1310–1510
78%	51%	1240–1440
75%	61%	1330
70%	46%	1360
79%	48%	27–30
85%	58%	24–29
67%	68%	1280
88%	51%	28–32
77%	42%	1180–2160
68%	63%	1340–1830, 19–25
79%	82%	24–29
82%	61%	25–30
83%	69%	1640–2010
87%	34%	1250–1430
78%	72%	1710–2050, 25–30
76%	53%	1750–2090
87%	35%	1240–1440
77%	73%	23–28
87%	30%	1280–1460
80%	63%	26–30
61%	74%	24–29
69%	68%	1040–1300
71%	61%	25–30
85%	53%	1430
82%	68%	26–31
71%	80%	23–28
NA	41%	28–32

COLLEGE	LOCATION	UNDERGRADUATE ENROLLMENT
University of Minnesota – Twin Cities	Minneapolis, MN	34,800 (large)
University of Notre Dame	Notre Dame, IN	8,500 (medium)
University of Wisconsin – Madison	Madison, WI	30,400 (large)
Wabash College	Crawfordsville, IN	910 (small)
Wheaton College	Wheaton, IL	2,400 (medium)

Southern Colleges and Universities

COLLEGE	LOCATION	UNDERGRADUATE ENROLLMENT
Agnes Scott College	Decatur, GA	870 (small)
Austin College	Sherman, TX	1,300 (small)
Baylor University	Waco, TX	12,600 (medium)
Birmingham Southern College	Birmingham, AL	1,300 (small)
Centre College	Danville, KY	1,300 (small)
Clemson University	Clemson, SC	15,700 (large)
College of William and Mary	Williamsburg, VA	6,100 (medium)
Eckerd College	St. Petersburg, FL	1,800 (small)
Emory & Henry College	Emory, VA	940 (small)
Georgia – Institute of Technology	Atlanta, GA	13,900 (medium)
Goucher College	Baltimore, MD	1,400 (small)
Guilford College	Greensboro, NC	2,700 (medium)
Hendrix College	Conway, AR	1,400 (small)
Lynchburg College	Lynchburg, VA	2,300 (medium)
McDaniel College	Westminster, MD	1,600 (small)
Millsaps College	Jackson, MS	910 (small)
New College of Florida	Sarasota, FL	850 (small)
Rhodes College	Memphis, TN	1,800 (small)
Southern Methodist University	Dallas, TX	6,200 (medium)
Southwestern University	Georgetown, TX	1,300 (small)
Spelman College	Atlanta, GA	2,200 (medium)
St. John's College	Annapolis, MD	490 (small)
Texas A&M University	College Station, TX	39,900 (large)

SIX-YEAR GRADUATION RATE	ADMISSIONS RATE	AVERAGE SAT/ACT SCORES (25TH–75TH PERCENTILE)
70%	47%	25–30
96%	24%	32–34
83%	51%	26–30
75%	63%	1260
87%	65%	27–32

SIX-YEAR GRADUATION RATE	ADMISSIONS RATE	AVERAGE SAT/ACT SCORES (25TH–75TH PERCENTILE)
65%	46%	1025–1260
75%	NA	NA
72%	40%	24–29
61%	NA	NA
82%	70%	1360
77%	63%	1140–1330
NA	35%	1240–1450
63%	68%	1230
48%	NA	NA
79%	51%	1260–1450
70%	73%	NA
58%	64%	1210
73%	83%	1360
52%	68%	1110
73%	75%	NA
66%	61%	1300
68%	56	1420
76%	49%	1200–1425
75%	55%	1180–1370
73%	65%	NA
77%	38%	945–1130
60%	78%	NA
80%	64%	1100–1300

COLLEGE	LOCATION	UNDERGRADUATE ENROLLMENT
University of Alabama	Tuscaloosa, AL	26,200 (large)
University of Florida – Gainesville	Gainesville, FL	32,000 (large)
University of Georgia	Athens, GA	26,400 (large)
University of Maryland – College Park	College Park, MD	26,800 (large)
University of Miami	Coral Gables, FL	10,500 (medium)
University of North Carolina – Chapel Hill	Chapel Hill, NC	18,400 (large)
University of Richmond	Richmond, VA	3,000 (medium)
University of South Carolina – Columbia	Columbia, SC	22,600 (large)
University of Texas – Austin	Austin, TX	38,400 (large)
University of Virginia	Charlottesville, VA	15,800 (medium)
Virginia Tech	Blacksburg, VA	23,700 (large)
Wake Forest University	Winston-Salem, NC	4,800 (medium)

SIX-YEAR GRADUATION RATE	ADMISSIONS RATE	AVERAGE SAT/ACT SCORES (25TH–75TH PERCENTILE)
66%	44%	22–29
84%	43%	1160–1360
83%	63%	1120–1310
82%	45%	1190–1400
78%	38%	1230–1400
90%	31%	1200–1400
83%	33%	1190–1390
70%	63%	1100–1290
81%	47%	1120–1380
NA	33%	1240–1460
82%	67%	1110–1310
88%	40%	1230–1400

RESOURCES

In the next few pages, you'll find links to all of the helpful resources that I mentioned throughout the book, handily collected into one place of reference. These resources will help you access information about specific colleges to inform your college list, apply for financial aid, learn more about standardized tests, and find quality academic summer programs for high school students. There are also some resources for students with learning disabilities and athletes who hope to get recruited by a college coach. Good luck with your research!

THE COMMON APPLICATION

Common Application • www.commonapp.org

COLLEGE SEARCH RESOURCES

College Board Search Engine • http://bigfuture.collegeboard.org

College Navigator from the National Center for Education Statistics •
http://nces.ed.gov/collegenavigator

College Confidential • www.collegeconfidential.com

College Prowler • www.collegeprowler.com

U.S. News & World Report • www.usnews.com/rankings

The Choice blog by the *New York Times* • http://thechoice.blogs.nytimes.com

The Princeton Review's 377 Best Colleges (Princeton Review, 2013)

Colleges That Change Lives: 40 Schools That Will Change the Way You Think About Colleges by Loren Pope (Penguin, 2012)

Colleges That Change Lives (CTCL) • www.ctcl.org

NEED-BASED FINANCIAL AID

Free Application for Federal Student Aid (FAFSA) • www.fafsa.ed.gov

FAFSA4Caster • http://FAFSA4caster.ed.gov

CSS Profile • http://profileonline.collegeboard.com

U.S. Department of Education Federal Student Aid Website • http://studentaid.ed.gov

State Higher Education Executive Officers (SHEEO) list of State Higher Education Agencies Contact Information • www.sheeo.org/agencies.asp

SCHOLARSHIPS

College Scholarships.org • www.collegescholarships.org

College Tool Kit • www.collegetoolkit.com

Fast Web • www.fastweb.com/college-scholarships

Financial Aid.Org • www.finaid.org/scholarships

Scholarship Experts.com • www.scholarshipexperts.com

Scholarships.com • www.scholarships.com

National Merit Scholarship Corporation • www.nationalmerit.org

Merit Aid.Com • www.meritaid.com

STANDARDIZED TESTING INFORMATION

College Board • www.collegeboard.org

ACT • www.actstudent.org

FREE TEST-PREP CLASSES

I Need a Pencil • www.ineedapencil.com

Let's Get Ready! • www.letsgetready.org

SUMMER PROGRAMS FOR HIGH SCHOOL STUDENTS

Enrichment Alley • http://enrichmentalley.com

Peterson's Summer Programs • www.petersons.com/
college-search/summer-programs-camps-search.aspx

THE NATIONAL COLLEGIATE ATHLETIC ASSOCIATION WEBSITE

National Collegiate Athletic Association (NCAA) • www.ncaa.org

RESOURCES FOR STUDENTS WITH LEARNING DISABILITIES

Learning Disabilities Association of America • www.ldanatl.org

National Center for Learning Disabilities • www.ncld.org

LD Online • www.ldonline.org

Attention Deficit Disorder Association • www.add.org

International Dyslexia Association • www.interdys.org

National Institute of Neurological Disorders and Stroke •
www.ninds.nih.gov

The K&W Guide to College for Students with Learning Disabilities by
Marybeth Kravetz and Imy Wax (Princeton Review, 2010)

ABOUT THE AUTHOR

Bea deGea © 2011

JOIE JAGER-HYMAN, EdD, is an internationally acclaimed expert on the college admissions process and the president and founder of College Prep 360 LLC, a full-service educational consulting company based in New York City that does both for-profit and nonprofit work. Her first book, *Fat Envelope Frenzy: One Year, Five Promising Students, and the Pursuit of the Ivy League Prize* (Harper Perennial, 2008), was recognized as one of the Ten Best Books of 2008 by the *Daily News Online*. As an expert on college admissions, Dr. Jager-Hyman has appeared on the *CBS Early Show*, *New England Cable News*, NPR, and dozens of other radio programs. She has also contributed to numerous publications, including *Forbes* and *New York*, on college admissions topics, has written research articles for academic journals and prominent policy reports, and has even testified at a congressional hearing on baccalaureate degree attainment. A graduate of Dartmouth College, Dr. Jager-Hyman served as assistant director of admissions for her alma mater, where she read and evaluated thousands of applications. She then went on to complete a doctorate in education policy at Harvard University, concentrating her research on the transition from high school to college.

Dr. Jager-Hyman is passionate about empowering parents and students around the world to make good decisions about education. She lives with her husband and son in Brooklyn, New York.

INDEX